$\mathcal{W}$RITING THAT $\mathcal{W}$ORKS

A Practical Guide for Business and Creative People

RICHARD ANDERSEN

McGRAW-HILL PUBLISHING COMPANY

New York   St. Louis   San Francisco   Bogotá
Hamburg   Madrid   Mexico   Milan   Montreal
Paris   São Paulo   Tokyo   Toronto

6 7 8 9 FGR FGR   9 2 1

ISBN 0-07-001693-3

Library of Congress Cataloging-in-Publication Data
Andersen, Richard
  Writing that works.
  Bibliography: p.
  Includes index.
  1. English language—Rhetoric. 2. English language—
Business English. 3. Creative writing. I. Title.
PE1408.A58 1989   808'.066651   88-13817
ISBN 0-07-001693-3

Book design by Eve Kirch

For Helene Hinis and Kathy Kraus

And for those who made
this book possible:
Dick and Helen Guilfoyle

CONTENTS

A word to the wise is not sufficient
if it doesn't make any sense.

—JAMES THURBER

$\mathcal{I}$NTRODUCTION

Do you ever sit down to write and all of a sudden—you don't know why or how or even when it happens—you find yourself standing in front of a vending machine?

Or do you ever sit down to write and suddenly you remember five or six absolutely crucial things that have to be done before you can put a single word on paper?

Or do you ever sit down to write and after ten or fifteen minutes you realize you've been daydreaming about the past weekend or the one coming up? So you get those daydreams out of your head and concentrate really hard on what you have to write, only nothing comes out? Not for ten, fifteen, twenty minutes, or however long it takes to be saved by your break for lunch?

After lunch you're ready to try again. The telephone stops ringing, your colleagues fall asleep, you've cleared your desk of anything that might distract you, and lo and behold, you manage to get a few words on the paper. Only they don't look right. Even if they were perfectly clear in your head, somehow, on paper, there's something wrong with them. A misplaced comma, a misspelled word, something. You tell yourself, "If I could only call this person on the phone, I could say in five seconds what it's taking me all day to write."

But you can't call, so you erase what you've written and start all over. The words still don't look right, but you have to live with them because time is running out. This memo or letter or article or whatever has to be off your desk in ten minutes or you shouldn't bother coming back to work on Monday.

Writing is not something most people find a whole lot of joy in. Even professional writers have trouble writing. Thomas Mann tells us, "A writer is a person for whom writing is more difficult than it is for other people." Joseph Jaubert writes, "To write well, one needs a natural facility and an acquired difficulty." Other writers are more direct. Novelist Gene Fowler tells us, "Writing is easy. All you have to do is sit down at a typewriter and wait for drops of blood to form on your forehead."

One of the reasons the writing process is so frustrating, sometimes even painful, has to do with the way we were taught to write. Because the truth is, we weren't taught to write. Our teachers called it writing, the books said "writing" on their covers, but what we learned wasn't writing. It was editing.

Remember the first grammar book you ever had? Remember the first lesson: "A noun is the name of a person, place, or thing"? We learned this definition and were then asked to pick out the nouns in a list of ten or twenty sentences. Then we went on to verbs. By the end of the book, we were wrestling with "who" and "whom." Some of us had even learned to diagram sentences.

But no matter how many rules we learned, no matter how many exercises we did, we still kept making mistakes. No matter how hard we tried, no matter how good our papers were, our teachers still found something wrong with them.

That was their job. If they couldn't find something wrong with everything we wrote, they'd failed. No wonder we had trouble!

If our parents had taught us to write, this book would never have been written. The things our parents accepted responsibility for, they really knew how to teach. What happens when a baby utters those first verbal sounds, "ma," "pa," or "da"? The parents go wild! They pick up baby, kiss baby, hug baby, tell baby how smart baby is, and more. Baby doesn't know what baby has done to deserve this attention, but it doesn't take long for baby to realize that every time baby says "ma," "pa," or "da," good things happen.

Unfortunately, we didn't learn to write this way. Instead of being encouraged to develop our own natural writing voices the way we developed our own individual speaking voices, we were taught to imitate other people's ways of writing. We were told these other people's ways were "correct," and we were given a set of grammatical rules to help us be "correct." No one ever mentioned "interesting." The result for many of us is a prose style that, even when "correct," is flat, dull, and turgid.

Consider these examples from published books and articles:

Signs are never static but are in a state of constant flux. Consequently, the specificity of any sign entails not only its difference from contemporaneous signs, but also its difference from temporally dispersed signifiers.

Operationally, teaching effectiveness is measured by assessing the levels of agreement between the perceptions of instructors and students on the rated ability of specific instructional behavior attributes which were employed during course instruction.

People with more favorable economic status have a significantly more favorable mortality experience than do people as a whole.

The main reason we tend to write this way is that we are insecure. Having had our mistakes pointed out to us in grammar school, high school, college, professional school, and all the years we've been working, we've never been able to develop any confidence in our ability to write. So what we've done instead is try to hide our insecurity behind big words and convoluted sentence structures. We learned to bully our readers so they wouldn't suspect how weak we were. Then we convinced ourselves that if they couldn't understand what we wrote it was because they were bad readers. We resolved not to lower our standards. And then, just to make sure the point sunk in, we created a word for the unintelligible garbage we created. We called it "professional."

This book takes us back to that point in time before deliberate obfuscation in compositional techniques became primarily impelled by enhanced professional status. In other words, it teaches us to write, not according to a set of rules and modes that have been imposed on us from without, but from the natural urge for self-expression we discovered when we first learned to speak. Once you have discovered your own individual, natural writing voice—the one that is as close as possible to the way you speak—you can use the rules and models of our language to create the kind of clear, easy-to-read prose that characterizes all good writing.

The process of learning to write naturally involves three steps: PREWRITING, FREEWRITING, and REWRITING.

That may seem like a lot to go through for a little memo or business letter. Especially if you've been taught to do it right the first time. But think for a minute how long it takes you now to write even a memo or a letter in one step. It takes so long because you're really trying to do three things simultaneously. You're trying to think of what you have to say, write it down, and get it correct, all at the same time. This is also why it's so hard to get started and why you're rarely satisfied with what you've written. What, in effect, you are doing is not much different from playing three different melodies all at one time on the piano. Imagine your left hand trying to play Mozart, your right hand trying to knock out some Gershwin, and your head banging away on some Cage or Wilson. To call what comes out "professional" makes about as much sense as calling a missile with nuclear warheads a "Peacekeeper."

By breaking this one big step with three parts into three separate steps to be completed one at a time, you'll discover two things right away: The time you usually spend writing will be cut in half, and the quality of your writing will improve dramatically. In the same time it takes people using traditional writing techniques to write their opening sentences, you will have completed the first two steps of the writing process presented in this book. Furthermore, this three-step process contains all the principles of good writing. Once you learn them—and the learning is easy, because they work the way our brains work naturally—you can apply them to anything you may wish to write: memo, letter, proposal, even an article, a short story, or a novel. The principles of good writing stay the same. Only the format changes.

As good as this new way of writing is, however, it can still be improved. It can still be fine-tuned to make a particular memo, letter, or report even more effective. That's where the rest of this book comes in. It shows you how to make prose that's clear, simple, and easy to understand even more lively, engaging, and powerful.

And you don't have to keep your head filled with a whole bunch of rules to do it! Writing correctly doesn't necessarily mean writing well. Nevertheless, guidelines and models conforming to traditional writing rules and accepted business practices are included—along with examples of how to successfully break almost every one of these rules. Just as this sentence did. In fact, almost every paragraph of this book contains examples of a rule observed or a rule broken. Sometimes both. The more you read, the clearer these examples will become to you.

Which brings me to the final point of this introduction.

If you follow the guidelines suggested in this book, your writing is going to improve. Right from the start. And it's going to continue to improve for some time afterwards. But somewhere along the line—maybe six months or a year and a half later—it's going to level off—and it's going to stay that way unless you supplement it with something else. You have to read. Anything. Books, magazines, newspapers, it doesn't matter. Reading is the best way for a writer to improve his or her style over a long period of time. Only don't read as a reader. Read as a writer. Readers read for pleasure and information. Writers read for pleasure and information too, but they also read for something else: techniques. Another writer, especially one in a different field, may have solved a particular problem that's baffled you for some time. Or another writer might introduce you to a new way of structuring a sentence, using a dash, or playing with a word. And don't feel bad about using someone else's techniques. It's a widely practiced form of flattery. Take whatever you can, and keep T. S. Eliot's advice close to your heart: "Amateurs plagiarize. Real writers steal."

—Richard Andersen
Amherst, Massachusetts

1

*P*REWRITING

HOW TO GET STARTED

> The best time for planning what you want to write is
> while you're doing the dishes.
> —*Agatha Christie*

No writer has ever lived who did not at some time have
trouble getting started. Charles Dickens used to stare for
hours at blank pages, afraid that if he left his desk he would
never return. Sir Walter Scott overcame writer's block by
writing something other than what he was supposed to
write. In fact, Scott rarely wrote anything that wasn't an
escape from something else.

Unfortunately, most of us lack Scott's resourcefulness or
Dickens' well-developed hindquarters. We need other kinds
of help.

Here are some suggestions for getting your words on
paper.

Think of Yourself as a Writer. Writers are people who
produce order out of chaos and communicate their dis-
coveries to others. Regardless of the kind of writing you
do, you are a writer. Your job is to communicate. And to
communicate effectively, you have to develop the courage
to be yourself, to put yourself on the line, to write as closely
as possible to the way you speak.

Know Your Subject. The more you know about your subject, the better you'll be able to write about it. It's as simple and as complex as that.

Know Your Reader. Knowing your reader is the next most important thing to knowing your subject. And for much the same reason. The better you know your reader, the more ways you'll have to influence him or her.

In *Techniques to Improve Your Writing Skills*, Bob Isles tells us that if we want our readers to agree with us, we need to know their views on the matter; if we're trying to increase their knowledge, we have to know what they already know; if we're trying to change the way something is done, we have to know why they use their present methods; and if we want action, we need to know what motivates them. In fact, we can make almost any communication more effective by allowing our readers' attitudes to determine what approach to take toward our subjects, what to include or leave out, and what methods of persuasion to use.

Ask yourself:

- What does my reader know?
- What does my reader need to know?
- What does my reader want to know?
- What does my reader think, feel, say, and do about my subject?

Knowing our readers so we can influence them doesn't mean we should deceive them, however. If we compromise our beliefs, oversimplify our points, or write only to confirm our readers' prejudices, we're going to lose their trust and respect. Lose these things and we lose everything. Without integrity, there is no communication.

Thinking of yourself as a writer, knowing your subject, and knowing your reader will go a long way toward helping you say what you want to say, but they still may not be enough to overcome writer's block. No one ever accused Dickens or Scott of not knowing their subjects or their audience, and Dickens and Scott probably never thought of themselves as anything other than writers. Yet they still had trouble getting their words down on paper.

Here are several techniques Dickens and Scott used to overcome writer's block, as well as some they would have liked to have known.

Set Aside Time to Write. If you're a morning person, find some time in the morning when you're least likely to be interrupted. You may wish to consider going to work early and completing your writing before everyone else arrives. An evening person may find working for an hour at home is more effective than struggling through the middle of an afternoon.

Perhaps you're a late-afternoon person, the kind who turns into a zombie about twenty minutes after lunch and stays that way until about an hour before it's time to go home. Then, in the last hour, you do all the work that's piled up since you got back from lunch. If you're this kind of person, you may wish to do all your writing in that last hour of the day. Not only do you have the energy then—you've slept most of the afternoon—you have something almost as important: a deadline. If you can get your writing done within that last hour, you get to go home.

Few things help writers get started faster than a deadline. Journalists, for example, rarely have trouble with writer's block. They don't have the time for it. They've got to cover a story, write it up, make whatever corrections are necessary, and get it to their editors all in one day. Many journalists claim that they write better under the pressure of a deadline. Instead of worrying about whether everything they write is grammatically correct, they're freed by the deadline to get their words on the paper. This act of writing faster gives their stories an energy they would otherwise lack.

Avoid Interruptions.   Few things shut down the writing process as quickly and as effectively as interruptions. Each one puts you back into the position of having to start all over again. So shut the door to your office, have your secretary hold your calls, and tell your colleagues you can't be interrupted for an hour.

Many people don't know or have forgotten what it's like to write. They think writing is the same thing as typing. You can just go back your desk and continue where you left off. You know different. You also know that most of us in the real world aren't so lucky as to have doors we can close, secretaries who'll hold our calls, and colleagues who are sensitive to our needs as writers.

So what can you do? If you have any influence where you work, you may wish to suggest a policy adopted at Hallmark Cards in Kansas City. Every employee is given a small flag on a stand. The flag is attached to its pole by strings that make the flag move up and down. Anytime anyone is working on something important and doesn't want to be interrupted, he or she places the flag at half staff. No one is allowed to interrupt until the flag goes up again. It's a simple policy, everyone knows it, and no doors, secretaries, or hurt feelings are involved.

Develop a Sense of Discipline.   Pliny puts this so well— *"Nulla dies sine linea"*—that writers from Anthony Trollope to John Updike have kept his words—"Not a day without a line"—in frames on their desks. William Goldman tells us, "The difference between me and the best writer you can think of and the worst writer you can name isn't that great in one sense: we all have the ability to sit down at our desks and not get up until we have some words down on paper." The key to successful writing depends not so much on talent as it does on discipline. Develop the discipline and this book will help you improve on whatever talent you have.

The best way to develop a sense of discipline is to do all your writing at the same time every day. For instance, instead of answering your memos and letters when you receive them or when you can get around to them, save them for the particular time you've set aside for writing. This will save you time and effort and also improve your writing.

And here's a way to read those memos and letters that will help you write better responses: Read them with a pen in your hand. Underline the most important parts. If a response to these parts comes to mind, write that response in the margin. That way, when you get down to writing your reply, you don't have to re-read a whole letter or memo, just the parts you've underlined. And if you've made a note to yourself in the margin, you know just where to begin your message.

What happens on the days when you have nothing to write? Write something anyway. Anything. A letter to a friend, an entry in a journal or diary, whatever. What you write is not so important as your writing at least ten minutes every working day. Make it a habit, like jogging or reading at night before you go to sleep. After a few weeks, you'll discover that if you miss your time to write you'll feel physically uncomfortable. Something's just not right. Make it right. Everything from getting started to improving your style will become easier.

Tell Someone What You're Trying to Say. Having a tough time organizing your ideas? Everything you write sound confused and confusing? Try saying to someone else what you want to say. Because we have confidence in our ability to speak, what we say is almost always clear and easy to understand. So tell a friend or colleague what you want to say. It won't take long, and most of the time, your message will be perfectly clear. The trick is to go back to your desk and write your message exactly as you said it.

Break the Material Down. Say you have five or six thoughts that refuse to go peaceably onto the paper. Write these thoughts onto a set of 3×5 cards, with one thought on each card. Then spread the cards out before you on your desk. Decide the order in which you want to present your ideas. This card/idea first, this card/idea second, and so on. Stack the cards according to your order. Now all you have to do is write from card to card, each card representing a separate paragraph or a separate section of whatever you write.

If the cards don't have to follow a chronological sequence or a step-by-step process, consider placing the card with the most important idea first and the one with the second most important idea last. Studies have shown that we tend to remember best what we read first and second best what we read last. How many of us, for example, remember the opening lines of Dickens' *A Tale of Two Cities*: "It was the best of times; it was the worst of times . . ."? Almost everybody. Even if we haven't read *A Tale of Two Cities*, we know the opening lines because they're so good people have not only remembered them, they've told them to others, and those others have passed them on, and the process has been repeated so many times since 1859, the lines have become a cliché.

What about the novel's closing lines? "It is a far, far better thing that I do now than I have ever done. It is a far better rest that I go to than I have ever known." How many of us remember them? Probably not as many as remember the opening lines, but can anyone remember any other lines in this 600-page novel?

Warm Up. A writer can warm up for writing the same way athletes warm up for sports: Stretch into it by doing the easy stuff first.

This advice comes from Ernest Hemingway, who began each writing day with two letters. That's what he needed to limber up for work on his stories.

Hemingway also knew how to end his writing day: in the middle of a sentence, in the middle of a paragraph. He discovered it was easier to get started the next day if he resumed his train of thought rather than have to think up a whole new one.

Write with One Person in Mind. Say you're writing to someone you don't know; you're having a hard time getting started. Pretend you're writing to your husband or wife or best friend. That will break the impersonal barrier that can exist between strangers, as well as help you write in a more natural tone of voice.

You can also use this technique when more than one person will read what you've written. For example, have you ever written a memo to six people and had three do exactly what you wanted while the other three did three completely different things?

This happens when not everyone knows what we know. Those who know what we know will do what we direct them to do; those who don't know what we know will do what they *think* we want them to do. By pretending to write to someone who knows less about the subject than anyone in the group—a husband or wife or best friend—we improve our chances of being understood by anyone who reads our messages.

Break the Pattern. If you usually write in the morning, try writing in the afternoon or in the evening, when your mind may be more relaxed. If you write on a computer terminal, switch to a pad and pencil; if you use a pencil, move to a typewriter; if you write on white paper, exchange it for some yellow.

Give Up. Sometimes, no matter how hard we try, the words just won't come. In fact, the harder we push, the less likely we are to pry anything loose. So back off. Do something else for a while—the more mindless the better—then come back to the writing.

HOW TO CLUSTER

> The truth is that productive, logical thinking, even in the most exact sciences, is far more closely related to the type of mind of the artist and the child than the ideal of the logician would lead us to suppose.
> —*Herbert Read*

The traditional way to create, organize, and record our thoughts is to outline them by numbers (1 . . . , 2 . . .) or by letters (a . . . , b . . .). The problem with this method is our brains don't work in horizontal or vertical lines. Outlines, like almost everything else that has to do with the way we were taught to write, have been imposed on our brains from without. Which is one reason why we hate to do them. The other is that they rarely seem to work very well.

What we need, then, is a method that allows our thoughts to emerge naturally and also enables us to record them in a clear, logical way.

Clustering is that method.

In *Writing the Natural Way*, Gabrielle Rico explains how outlining forces us to think, record, and order our thoughts simultaneously. The experience is not much different from trying to keep three oranges in the air at the same time. It can be done, but it takes a lot of time and practice, and it limits us to the few thoughts we can juggle at any one time.

Clustering breaks this one step with three parts into four steps to be taken one at a time. Clustering enables us to hold off our logical, outline-oriented consciousness long enough to record the creative, lightning-fast associations our minds are capable of.

All we need is a piece of paper, a pen or pencil, and a word.

STEP #1: Write in the middle of a blank page the name of the person, place, product, service, or idea you want to write about.

STEP #2: Draw a circle around the word you've written in the center of the paper.

STEP #3: Sit back and relax. This is probably the most important step in clustering, the key to making the whole process work. Allow your mind to go with whatever thoughts your subject inspires. Don't try to think of things to say; let them come naturally into your mind.

STEP #4: Record these thoughts in one or a few words. Circle each thought as it is written down and draw a line from that thought to the one that inspired it.

For example, suppose I wanted to devote a section of this book to some of the ways clustering can help you write better. I might begin by writing "The Advantages of Clustering" in the middle of a blank page and circling it (see Figure 1).

Then I'd relax and let my mind wander over all the reasons I like to cluster. The first reason that came to mind might be that it's fast: I can cluster almost any letter I need to write in less than two minutes. It's also easy: I can forget

THE ADVANTAGES OF CLUSTERING

Figure 1

Figure 2

about being logical, I don't have to worry about spelling, grammar, or punctuation, and I can let my mind go in any direction it pleases. In fact, I've come up with more creative solutions to my problems *after* I've begun clustering than at any other time. Now, if I had clustered what I just wrote, my paper would look like Figure 2.

My next set of clusters might take the shape shown in Figure 3. "Hand/Mind" and "No lost thoughts" may not mean much to you, but I know what they mean, and when it comes to clustering, that's all who matters. Clusters don't have to be neat; they just have to make sense to their creator.

"Hand/Mind," to me, means that my hand can finally keep up with my mind. Have you ever found yourself writing one thought when another one comes into your mind? But you have to finish writing down the first thought before you can begin writing the second one? And by the

Figure 3

time you finish writing the first thought, you've forgotten the second one? And no matter how hard you try, you can't get the second thought back again? And the second thought is usually ten times better than the first?

That happens to me all the time. Or it used to, until I started clustering. Now I'm able to capture *all* my thoughts, because I don't have to write any of them out in complete sentences.

Figure 4 shows some more reasons why I like to cluster. Sometimes when you cluster, you may feel as if you're wandering aimlessly. Don't let that bother you. It's just your conditioned desire to be logical wanting to see everything

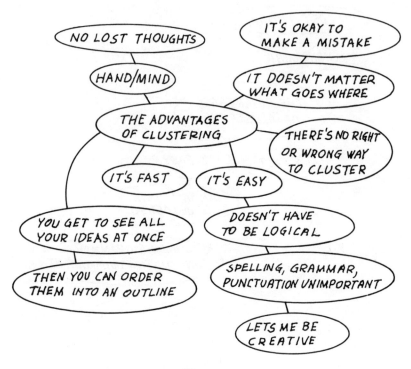

Figure 4

in terms of an outline. After you're familiar with the natural process of clustering—natural because it works the way our minds work—that initial anxiety will disappear. It may even be replaced with a sensation similar to playfulness.

Now, what do you do if your cluster looks like Figure 5, or like Figure 6? In the case of Figure 5, which is the more common, see if you can combine some of your clusters into one cluster; in the case of Figure 6, see if you can divide each big cluster into two or more smaller ones. Remember: When it comes to clustering, nothing is fixed; anything can be changed once your thoughts are on the paper. And you can still add any thoughts that come to mind while you're

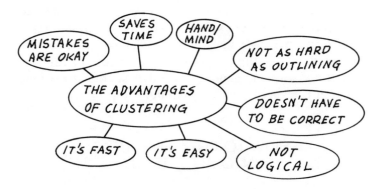

Figure 5

playing with the thoughts you've already recorded. You can also cross out the ideas you don't want to use or you find redundant. What you end up with may look like a mess, but, once again, you're the only one your clusters have to make sense to.

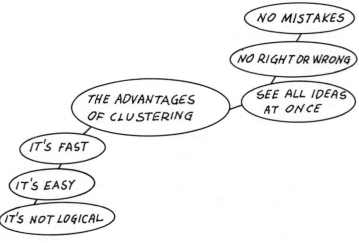

Figure 6

And how about the time you run out of ideas? How do you overcome clusterer's block? Try doodling with the clusters. Trace over the lines and draw arrows between the circles. Relaxing this way—instead of *trying* to think of something—usually generates another set of associations.

When you feel you've said enough, stop.

HOW TO ORGANIZE IDEAS
INTO AN OUTLINE

Writing is all a matter of choice and arrangement.
—*Graham Greene*

Take an overall look at what you've clustered. Some of it may not make sense. That's okay. Wisdom has nothing to do with logic. Your mind knows where you're going, even if you don't. Nevertheless, an outline, or at least the beginning and end of one, can probably be visualized from what you've clustered. The trick is to let your mind do the work for you.

Try to see each set of clusters as a separate paragraph. Choose the cluster that contains the most important information—the information you want your reader to remember best. Mark that cluster with the letter *B*. Mark with a letter *E* the cluster which contains the second most important piece of information—the information you want to end with. Then order the remaining clusters in between.

If I were going to outline my clusters on the advantages of clustering, I'd probably put a *B* next to "It's fast," because the sooner I get my writing over with, the sooner I get to play basketball, go to a movie, read a book, lie in the sun, eat a croissant with jam, and more. I'd probably end my outline with "You get to see all your ideas at once," because that helps me outline faster, and faster outlining also saves me time for things I like to do better. Then I'd number

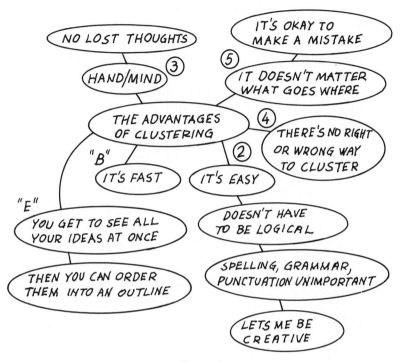

Figure 7

the remaining clusters in the order I planned to use them. Now my cluster looks like Figure 7.

If you were ordering this cluster into an outline, you might have begun or ended with a different set of clusters. That's okay. When it comes to choosing the most important and second most important pieces of information, whatever you choose will become the most important and second most important pieces of information. Let your intuition dictate your choices. It won't fail you. In fact, your enthusiasm for what you choose almost guarantees your choices are the right ones.

Most of the time, you'll be able to write from the outline

you've created on your set of clusters. Simply begin your first paragraph with the information listed in the cluster marked *B*. Then move on to the second paragraph of your memo or letter with the information clustered in #2.

If, however, your cluster has become confused because of too many changes, you may want to list your points in a traditional outline form. My cluster on the advantages of clustering would then look like this:

B. It's fast.

2. It's easy. You don't have to be logical, you don't have to worry about spelling, grammar, or punctuation, and you can free your mind to come up not only with more creative solutions to your problems but with more creative ways of articulating them.

3. Now your hand can keep up with your mind. No more forgetting one thought because you've had to write down another.

4. There's no right or wrong way to cluster. Whatever works best for you is best.

5. It doesn't matter what goes where on the paper because clustering works the way our minds work: not in outlines but with our thoughts scattered all over the page.

6. Once our thoughts are out of our heads and down on paper where we can see them, we can begin to order them into an outline.

This is a good outline for ordering our ideas and making sure we've included all we want to say, but it's not the only way to order our thoughts. Once we've clustered all our thoughts on any particular subject, we can order them from the least to the most important, from the general to the particular, from the personal to the universal, from the causes to the effects, or however else the subject may dictate. Donald Hall, in *Writing Well*, suggests an outline that is ordered the same way as a relay team: the second best first, the third best second, the weakest third, with the best being saved for last.

All of these outlines have an advantage over the traditional outline form of introduction, body, and conclusion because they have not been overused. They also include other advantages. In the traditional outline, much of what you were taught to say in the introduction is already known to the reader. This not only wastes the reader's time, it leads him or her to believe that your message contains nothing new. The reader is tempted to throw away your message before reaching the new information. In the outline constructed from the cluster, however, you present the most important information in the first paragraph. The reader is involved in your message right from the beginning.

And the body of your message, unlike the traditional list of details or ideas that often don't seem to lead anywhere, keeps the reader involved. It builds point upon point, adding new information in each paragraph, arriving at a conclusion that replaces the traditional repetitious summary with an inspired springboard to action: Start Clustering.

HOW CLUSTERING CAN HELP YOU IN WAYS THAT HAVE NOTHING TO DO WITH WRITING

In most lives insight has been accidental. We wait for it as primitive man awaited lightning for a fire. But making mental connections is our most crucial learning tool, the essence of human intelligence: to forge links; to go beyond the given; to see patterns, relationship, context.

—*Marilyn Ferguson*

Clustering reflects the way our minds work naturally. Yet we all have a tendency to reject the unconventional. No matter how frustrating or painful our traditional writing practices may be, at least we're familiar with them. We know their limits. And this business of drawing circles on a piece of paper seems, by comparison, childish or even stupid.

Give clustering a chance. Try not to resist a process that will bring significant changes not only to your writing but to your creative powers as well. In fact, clustering can influence your life in many ways that have little or nothing to do with writing.

Solve a Problem. And you can do it individually or in a group. For group work, have one person cluster on a board or overhead projector any solutions that may be offered. Once everyone's solutions are where they can be seen all at once, the group can begin refining them.

Dictate a Letter. One of the toughest things about dictating a letter is keeping the whole message in mind as you move from paragraph to paragraph. By clustering the letter beforehand, you can determine which parts you wish to say in what order, and can focus more fully on each part before moving on to the next. And you never lose sight of the whole because it's right there in front of you the whole time.

Evaluate a Product, Service, or Idea. Say you're asked to write a letter of recommendation or evaluate someone for a promotion. Write the person's name in the middle of a blank piece of paper and cluster whatever comes to mind. You'll be surprised how effectively clustering can rekindle your memory and generate new ideas.

You can also cluster all the advantages and disadvantages of that new computer your boss has asked you to use for a month. And here's a tip for when you write your report:

Instead of listing all the advantages in one section and all the disadvantages in another section, see if you can't divide your report into categories. Each category could be one paragraph listing the computer's advantages and disadvantages within the context of that category.

Take Notes at a Meeting or in a Class. We all know how difficult it is to take notes and listen at the same time. Trying to do two jobs at once, we wind up doing each half as well. Now, through clustering, we can record in a few notes whatever is spoken and devote the best part of our time to listening.

When exam time comes, students who have clustered their professors' lectures can review each lecture from the single page on which it was clustered. And because they were able to listen, their memories don't fail them when they review each cluster.

Make a List of Things You Have to Do. Have you ever come to work after a three-day weekend or a vacation to find your desk so overrun with memos, letters, phone messages, and more that you don't know where to begin? Try clustering all the tasks before you. Not only will you be able to categorize them into clusters that will save you time and energy, you'll also be able to determine in what order you want to tackle them.

Clustering can also help you run errands. After clustering all you need to do, categorize your clusters into areas where several things can be done at once. For example, you might be able to pick up stationery at a store near the photocopy center you have to go to, or perhaps while you're at the post office you can buy the mailing envelopes you would have ordinarily bought somewhere else. And if you number these places in the order you want to go to them, you won't find yourself traveling from one end of town to the other and then back again.

You can also use clustering to establish goals and plan projects. Psychologists use clustering to help their patients handle stress. Once whatever is causing the anxiety has been clustered, it can be put into a perspective, and the next step toward a resolution can be taken. In fact, psychologists have discovered that some stress is relieved simply by the act of being able to see the problem from the advantage of an overview that clustering makes possible.

The police now use clustering to interrogate suspects. As one officer asks a list of predetermined questions, another clusters the physical responses made by the suspect. Later, the responses are compared with the questions and a whole new set of questions is made up, based on what the suspect may have revealed through his or her behavior.

In short, once you develop the habit of clustering, you'll discover more and more ways it can be used. The applications are as unlimited as life itself.

2

$\mathcal{F}$REEWRITING

HOW TO DO IT

By the time anyone learns to write he has already learned how to speak in rather complex ways, and in most schools it is presumed that writing must be taught almost as something totally different from speaking.
—*Roger Sale*

The best writing technique there is—the one the pros use—is called "freewriting." Nothing helps you get words on paper faster; nothing can give your sentences more power or energy. Learn to freewrite and not only will your prose become more lively and engaging, you'll never have trouble getting started again. Freewriting makes writer's block history.

Here's an example of how much freewriting can help you. Whitney Smith was a promising reporter at the Memphis *Commercial Appeal* when he learned to freewrite. He had a master's degree in journalism from Ohio State University and five years of experience in newspapers, but his writing style rarely had more punch to it than this:

> The Jackson Symphony Association has hired Dr. Jordan Tang, a composer and former maestro of several orchestras, as its new music director and conductor. He will make his local debut at the Jackson Civic Center this July 19th.

Dr. Tang, 38, will meet local arts patrons today in Jackson. He comes from North Carolina, where he has been associate conductor of the Charlotte Symphony and the Charlotte Pops Orchestra for three years. Before that, he taught for five years at Southwest Missouri State University in Springfield, Missouri, and conducted the Ozark Festival Orchestra there.

A native of Hong Kong, Dr. Tang is a graduate of the Chinese University there. He moved to the United States in the late 1960s. He has a master's degree in church music. . . .

Had enough? There are only two people in the whole world who could read this story to its end: Whitney Smith's mother and Jordan Tang's mother. Every comma is in its place, all the facts are logically presented, but the effect isn't much different from taking Sominex.

When Whitney rewrote this story using freewriting techniques, he discovered he could not only put life into a dull subject, he could write twice as much in less than a third of the time.

And listen to the difference:

There are people in Jackson, Tennessee, who think Jordan Tang is a fish out of water.

Here's a guy with Chinese ancestry and a Ph.D. in music swimming around in what, artistically speaking, is a pretty small pond.

But Tang, who will open his first full season with the Jackson Symphony this July 19th, figures he can make a big splash.

"I would like to see more concerts, a slightly bigger orchestra, a larger audience, some major works, and, as a result, a bigger budget," Tang said. "I think we have lots of potential; we just need lots of support." . . .

Whitney's first version of this story, which was less than 200 words long, took 6½ hours to complete. Freewriting the second version, he wrote 1,000 words in less than an hour. And notice how much more quickly the second version reads even though there's not much difference in the length of the two excerpts.

Freewriting, like clustering, is based on the theory that our brains are divided into two parts: the left side and the right side. The left side thinks logically from one point to the next. Like a computer, it draws on a predetermined set of rules and procedures. Making sure we don't end any of our sentences in prepositions, for example, is a predominantly left-side brain activity. The right side, on the other hand, is neither logical nor linear. The impulsive, unconventional, and creative mark its territory. Instead of processing our thoughts literally, the brain's right side responds to words in terms of the images they evoke. This is why, for example, we can recall the words to a song if we sing it right through from beginning to end but have a hard time continuing if we're interrupted or can't remember a particular line unless we sing the song through from the beginning.

Obviously the two halves are complementary. Without the left side of our brains, our world would be chaos; without the right, our lives would be so rigid and predictable, original thinking would be almost impossible. Together, however, they produce the kind of experience we enjoy when, reading a book, we begin visualizing the plot and characters. It's almost as if we create in our minds a movie of what we're reading. The pages go by so quickly, we're hardly aware of turning them, and when we finally look at a clock, we can't believe how many minutes have flown by.

Unfortunately, we weren't taught how to use the right side of our brains when we write. Rather than be creative, we focus on correctly spelled words and prefabricated sentence structures. Freewriting gives us the balance we never allowed between the brain's creative right side and its controlling left side. One result is the difference between Whitney's first story about Jordan Tang and his second. When the right side of Whitney's brain got into the act of writing, Jordan Tang came alive in our imagination in ways that weren't possible before.

Here's how to make your prose come alive through freewriting:

Set a Time Limit. No less than five minutes but no more than fifteen. You could probably write longer—an hour or two if you had to—but the quality of your writing would be uneven, and you probably wouldn't have a good time doing it. The advantage to writing for only five, ten, or fifteen minutes at a time is that you get the writing over with quickly. Then you can reward yourself with a cup of coffee, a walk around the office, or a nice long stare at the ceiling before writing for another five, ten, or fifteen minutes.

Studies show that we write better when we take frequent but short breaks. So write for the number of minutes you're most comfortable with, break for a few minutes, then return to your writing for another short but productive roll. Just because you don't have a pen in your hand every minute doesn't mean you aren't writing. In fact, some writers claim they do their best writing before they ever pick up a pen.

Write Nonstop. "Nonstop" is the crucial word here. Because of the way we were taught to write, we tend to write down a few words and then stare at them. Somehow, no matter how clear these words may have been in our minds, they often don't look right on paper. A comma is missing, or perhaps we misspelled a word. No sooner have we started writing than we also begin editing.

Today we know that writing and editing are two separate brain functions: Writing is a predominantly right-side activity, while editing is predominantly left-side. We also know that old habits are hard to break. That's where freewriting comes in. By forcing ourselves to write nonstop for five, ten, or fifteen minutes, we push through our conditioned impulse to edit.

So once you start freewriting, don't stop. Not even for a second. Open the gates. Let the words pour out onto the page. Take some risks now, when there are no penalties. What comes out may sometimes be bad, but freewriting is the best technique for producing something really good. If you can't think of anything to say, write, "I can't think of anything to say. I can't think of anything to say. I can't think of anything to say." You'll think of something to say. Anything will be better than writing "I can't think of anything to say" more than three times.

Write Quickly. The whole purpose of freewriting is to limit the influence of your brain's left side and free the creative energies of the right side. Writing as quickly as you can helps this process. And don't worry if you make mistakes. The purpose of freewriting is not the product; it's to experience the process.

Forget About Spelling, Grammar, and Punctuation. These are left-side brain activities. Resist them. A misspelled word, an awkwardly constructed sentence, a forgotten comma—they won't go away. And they'll look just as bad later as when you first wrote them down. The time for editing will come soon enough. What you want to do now is write. The minute you stop to correct something, the left side of the brain has won out and you have to begin all over again the process of trying to open up the right side of your brain.

Let Your Mind Go. Freewriting is for you. Forget about what anyone else might think. Let your pen or typewriter or word processor record wherever your mind may lead you, even if your thoughts don't make much sense or don't come out in complete sentences. You'll discover with time and practice that these thoughts have their value. Some of them may not apply immediately to the task at hand, but you'll use them eventually. Which is the second reason why you don't want to erase words, cross them out, replace them with others, re-read them before you're through, or throw them all in the wastepaper basket (the first reason is that these activities shut off the right side of our brains).

John Simon, a nineteen-year-old student at the University of Massachusetts, freewrote this paragraph in just a few minutes:

When I first saw it I wasn't impressed. The paint was dull, the interior was dirty, and the noise reminded me of a freight train. I had been waiting all week for it to arrive, I had never been in one, and my father had told oh so many stories about these wonderful cars, Well, there it was in my driveway. Finally. I turned and walk back into my house. Understand, please, that this wasn't my car. If it had been, I sure as hell wouldn't have been in the house. The car, you see, was to be my sister's.

You try it. For five minutes, write *nonstop* about anything that comes into your mind. If you can complete half a page in that time, you've done well. Anything more than half a page in five minutes is excellent.

Now what happens if, at the end of five minutes, you haven't reached that point in your writing where the right side of your brain has taken over? The words aren't coming by themselves, and you're still trying to think of something to say?

Don't worry about it. You're probably acting on residual

impulses from the left side of your brain. Such as thinking. Nothing blocks writers as effectively as thinking. It throws them off the same way an athlete's thinking what he's going to do once he has caught a ball almost always makes him drop it.

Also, don't be afraid to give yourself another chance. It's rarely taken anyone more than ten minutes to experience the energy of freewriting and, once you know the feeling, it's like swimming or riding a bike: you never forget. You'll also discover that each time you freewrite, it will take you less and less time to release the right-side brain energies. Good freewriters—those who practice for at least five minutes every day—can open the right sides of their brains in less than a minute.

HOW TO FREEWRITE FROM A CLUSTER

> For constructing any work of art you need some principle of repetition or recurrence; that's what gives you rhythm in music and pattern in painting.
> —*Northrop Frye*

Pick a subject. If you don't have something screaming to be written about, choose a topic you're interested in. Or one you can relax and have some fun with: an upcoming vacation, the sports team you love to hate, a favorite saying or emotion, a dream or story you read recently, your best or worst boss.

Now write in the middle of a blank piece of paper the name of the person, place, product, service, or idea you've chosen to write about.

Draw a circle around the word you've written in the center of the paper.

Now the most important part: Sit back and relax. Don't

think. Instead, cluster onto your paper whatever thoughts come into your minds about the subject you've chosen.

When you've finished, mark with the letter *B* the cluster you think is your best one, the one you want your reader to remember most. Mark your second best cluster, the one you want to end your exercise, with the letter *E*.

Now number all your other clusters in the order you wish to write about them.

Charlotte Thomas, an administrative assistant with the Physicians Insurance Company of Ohio, made up the cluster in Figure 8 about a former boss in less than two minutes. She then freewrote everything that came into her mind about what was in the first cluster. When there was nothing left to say, and *only* when there was nothing left to say, did she move on to freewriting everything that came into her mind about what was in the second cluster. She also wasn't

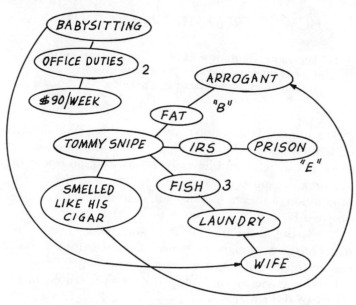

Figure 8

shy about including anything that wasn't in the clusters, because she knew she could always come back later and cross out whatever was irrelevant. In other words, Charlotte followed the basic structure set up by the clusters, but she didn't let it hinder her from freewriting anything that came into her mind.

Here's what came out:

Tommy Snipe was the worst boss I ever had. He was a fat, sloppy, arrogant, pompous, ill-mannered man who made a lot of noise and smelled like his cigar.

Snipe paid me $90 a week. My job duties included typing, shorthand, bookkeeping, handling clients—the usual office duties—plus babysitting for his three-year-old daughter Mindy while performing all of the above clerical tasks of course, cleaning his aquarium every week (which was home for tropical fish he treated better than most people) taking his suits to the dry-cleaners—He would throw stacks of dirty laundry on top of whatever I was working on at my desk. And consoling his wife who called at least five times a day with various crises: the washer broke, the cow got out, Mindy wouldn't behave, etc.

For Christmas, Snipe gave me a recycled card; I gave him leather gloves costing half a week's salary.

Then the IRS found out that Snipe was using illegal trust funds to put his three kids through school. He's now serving time in a federal prison for income tax evasion.

As a going away gift my last day on the job, I flushed his tropical fish down the toilet. I told him they'd died, they had. I explained to the fish it was something I had to do. They understood. They didn't like him either.

And the time it took Charlotte to write this essay? Five minutes.

HOW FREEWRITING HELPS YOU

> There is in writing the constant joy of sudden discovery, of happy accident.
>
> —*H. L. Mencken*

Freewriting Gets Our Thoughts on Paper. Especially when combined with clustering. Think for a minute how much time and energy you now spend not writing but worrying about what you're going to say, how you're going to say it, and if you're going to say it correctly. Freewriting takes you past these obstacles to where you need to be: writing.

Once you have your words on paper, you can change them around and make sure they're correct. Not only will you be able to do this work faster and more easily than before, you'll be able to do it without losing any of the natural energy your freewriting has pumped into it.

Freewriting Gets Us Started. Fast. Instead of wasting time and effort procrastinating, staring at a blank page, or trying to think of the best words to begin with (the Constipated School of Writing), just freewrite. You know that your writing almost always goes more smoothly and comes out better once you've begun. So start freewriting and don't worry if what you've written is good or bad. When you're finished, you'll have plenty of time to go back and rewrite your opening sentence. In fact, studies have shown that many writers can cluster *and* freewrite before those using traditional techniques can get even a single word on paper.

And the opening sentence you rewrite *after* you've finished freewriting will not only take you less than a couple of minutes, it will often be twice as good as any you could have come up with, had you tried to think of a satisfactory beginning before going on to your second sentence. Charlotte's opening sentence about her boss, for example, reads: "Tommy Snipe was the worst boss I ever had." After freewriting her essay, she went back and changed the sentence to read: "Tommy Snipe was a small-town attorney with a big-city ego."

Freewriting Makes Writing Easier. Even when you don't feel like doing it. Because freewriting doesn't have to be "correct," it relieves much of our anxiety about writing. And because it's so fast and powerful, freewriting helps us get our writing over with sooner.

Freewriting Helps Us Think of Things to Write About. Compare Charlotte's cluster with her essay. Look how many more things came into her mind when she freewrote than when she clustered. Clustering got her initial thoughts down on paper so she could see them all at once and organize them, but freewriting enabled Charlotte to develop them into engaging, lively, effective, powerful prose.

Freewriting Helps Us Be More Creative. When you freewrite, you are as close to your conscious stream of thoughts as writing can take you. Opening up the right side of your brain, freewriting helps you discover more imaginative ways of saying what you want to say. You'll find yourself grabbing your reader's attention in ways you never could have anticipated.

Charlotte provides us with a good example of this kind of creativity when she tells us: "For Christmas, Snipe gave me a recycled card; I gave him leather gloves costing half a week's salary."

That line is so sad and so well placed in the story, it creates what writers call a "dramatic tension" between the terrible things Snipe does to Charlotte and Charlotte's revenge at the end. When those fish go down the toilet, we are on Charlotte's side in a way we would never have been if Snipe hadn't given her the recycled card and she hadn't spent a half week's salary on leather gloves for him. Or to put it another way, imagine what this story would have been like if it had begun with the fish going down the toilet. We would think, What kind of person would flush tropical fish down a toilet? And no matter what Charlotte said afterwards, we would never be as much on her side as we are now. By saving the flushing for the end and preceding it with the sadness of the card and gloves, Charlotte has us emotionally right where she wants us. We still may not know what kind of person flushes tropical fish down a toilet, but we have a pretty clear idea of what kind of person would drive someone to flush tropical fish down a toilet.

Master craftsmen spend years learning how to create dramatic tension; Charlotte accomplished the same feat through freewriting. She wasn't aware of what she'd done, and we won't be able to scale such heights every time we write, but we can appreciate the authenticity and color freewriting brings to Charlotte's prose. Discussing these qualities in her book *The Executive Memo*, Sherry Sweetnam tells us the great advantage of freewriting is that it helps bridge the gap between the real you—the person your readers want to hear from—and the business you—the person you think your readers want to hear from.

Freewriting Improves Our Writing. Even when freewriting doesn't produce the kind of writing we discovered in Charlotte's story about Tommy Snipe, it still leads to powerful writing because it helps you get out of the words' way. It allows your thoughts to create their own means of expression without having to suffer the corrections the left side of your brain is dying to impose upon them.

Have you ever read something that was fluent and clear and correct and to the point but hopelessly boring? Writers who write this way exercise too much control over the language. They take away its power and kill it. Good writers, on the other hand, allow their subjects to determine the way the writing goes. Good writers have confidence in their subjects' words. They know it's the words that energize the writer, not the other way around. Listen to the power of the sound in these words by John Updike: "What soul took thought and knew that adding 'wo' to man would make a woman? The difference exactly. The wide w. The receptive o. Womb. . . . Seven years since I wed wide warm woman, white-thighed. Wooed and wed. Wife. A knife of a word that for all its final bite did not end the wooing. To my wonderment."

Freewriting Prepares Us for the Next Step in the Writing Process: Rewriting. Freewriting gives us something to work with: words, sentences, paragraphs. You may throw as many as half of them away, but it is easier to cut and change and correct when those words are on the paper in front of you than it is to create and correct them while they're still in your head. And because you were able to freewrite quickly and without much effort, you won't resist changing your words as much as if you had devoted a lot of time and energy to getting them down on paper. In fact, you freewrite knowing you will make changes. Freewriting gives your prose imagination and energy; rewriting makes it shine.

3

REWRITING

WHAT THE PROS DO

What makes me happy is rewriting. In the first draft you get your ideas and your theme clear, if you are using some kind of metaphor you get that established, and certainly you have to know where you're coming out. But the next time through it's like cleaning house, getting rid of all the junk, getting things in the right order, tightening things up. I like the process of making writing neat.

—*Ellen Goodman*

Many of us see rewriting as a sign of failure. Because we've been told that if we can come up with a good opening sentence the rest of what we write will take care of itself, we think we've made a mistake when we come across something we didn't cover in our opening sentence. And because we've been taught that if we do something right the first time we won't have to go over it again, we've come to believe a good writer is someone who can sit down and, after a few minutes reflection, crank out a perfect letter or report or article on his or her first try.

People like Vladimir Nabokov know better: "I never had a pencil that outlived its eraser," he once wrote. And James Michener agrees. He knows that freewriting only *sounds* good. "I'm probably the world's worst writer," he said in an interview. "But I'm the world's best rewriter."

Nevertheless, there are ways to keep our rewriting time to a minimum.

Know Your Subject.   Not knowing your subject well enough often results in cloudy thinking. And cloudy thinking leads to cloudy writing. How many times have you wandered through a memo or letter having little or no idea where you were heading? Know your subject well enough to say clearly whatever it is you want to say. The message you don't want your reader to receive is the one that you don't know what you're talking about or don't know enough to think clearly about it.

Know Your Reader.   So often we assume that our readers have the same point of view or body of knowledge that we do. This leads us to omit information that is second nature to us but may be crucial to our readers, who wind up either confused by what they don't know or hostile about having to translate what they don't understand.

A good example of this kind of writing appears in almost anything printed by bureaucrats in large governments. These people rarely consider their readers' points of view because they don't have to. With all the power on their side, they have to write only for themselves.

We don't have that luxury. Not only must we know our readers' viewpoints, we must respect them for effective communication to take place.

Respecting our readers, however, doesn't mean writing to impress them with big words or long sentences. That only alienates them. The purpose of effective communication is not to *im*press but to *ex*press.

Organize Your Thoughts.   Clustering and, if need be, outlining should take you the distance here, but just to be sure, ask yourself:

- What am I trying to say?
- Did I say it clearly in a sentence or two?
- Are my ideas presented in a logical order?
- Did I leave something out?
- What questions will my reader ask now?

THE FAST WAY

> Words are like leaves, and where they most abound,
> Much fruit of sense beneath is rarely found.
> —*Alexander Pope*

Rewriting the fast way gives you a clean, easy-to-read piece of writing when you don't have time for a major revision. Here's what to do.

Check the Overall Flow

Don't try to find your mistakes and correct them one at a time. You'll work faster and more effectively if you read your memo or letter as a whole. Make sure it's easy to read. There should be no words that will send anyone running to the dictionary or sentences that will make their eyes glaze over.

Now you're ready for the particulars. Read through your memo or letter several times, each time focusing on a smaller element. Start with the paragraphs and work your way down through the sentences, phrases, and words.

The Paragraphs.   Make sure each paragraph flows logically into the next. Does each paragraph build point upon point until an inevitable conclusion is reached?

Many writers try to raise a question in their readers' minds toward the end of one paragraph and answer it at the beginning of the next. There are two advantages to this technique:

1. Your readers are more actively engaged in what they are reading.

2. You don't have to create any transitions because your readers make all the transitions in their minds.

The result is good reading as well as good writing.

The Sentences. As you did with the paragraphs, make sure each sentence flows logically into the next. Also, generally speaking, short sentences tend to be more effective than long sentences. But length doesn't matter so much as each sentence's saying clearly what you want it to say.

The Phrases. Some clichés, jargon, and bureaucratic phrases may be all right when we're writing to someone in our field, but good writers will eliminate as many of them as they can. Good writers recognize these phrases as signs of a lazy imagination. They also know that many memos and letters are read by people other than the ones they were written for, and if these people don't understand our jargon, we're going to come off as bad writers. Few people think of themselves as poor memo or poor letter readers. Try, then, to "judge" rather than "adjudicate." See if you can "order" instead of "enjoin." "Get" as easily as you "procure." And do it "now" instead of "at this point in time."

The Words. We have many words to choose from when we write, but there are many things we don't have—eye contact, gestures, facial expressions, and vocal inflections, to name a few. So we have to make every word count. We have to find the right words to say what we want to say because we know that the right words communicate. Wrong ones confuse. Mark Twain tells us that the difference between the right word and the almost-right word is the difference between the lightning and the lightning bug.

How do you know when you have the right word? Examine the content. Have you allowed the content to determine its own means of expression? Those words the content inspires in our hearts and minds are the lightning words. Charlotte Thomas, for example, did not have to go to a thesaurus to to write "Tommy Snipe was a small-town attorney with a big-city ego." She found those words in the way Tommy Snipe treated her.

Finally, make sure you've spelled all those lightning words correctly. They may be clear in your heart, but your dictionary will help you make sure they're clear on paper as well.

Check the Opening Sentence

The opening sentence may be the most important sentence we write. Studies tell us that if we don't capture our reader's attention in the first five or ten seconds of whatever we write, one of two things happens: Either our beautiful prose, which we struggled so hard to perfect, winds up in the round file, or if our readers *have* to read what we've written, they won't give it their full attention.

How do we know when we've written an opening that grabs the reader's attention? We know. We know the same way we know whether anything we read is good: If we like it, it's good; if we don't, it isn't.

Take a look at the following opening sentences. Which one is better?

The Danubian Basin, which serves as the locus for this narrative, is a relatively closed geographical unit which began to change rapidly toward the end of the eighteenth century, under the impact of forces at work within the core area of the rising global economic system.

He was the kind of kid who only got Valentines from those whose mothers made them send one to everyone.

No question which is better. The first is long, confusing, wordy, dull, and impersonal; the second is just the opposite.

Here are some business openings:

I know a radical from Berkeley who holds the stock market in contempt but refuses to sell his shares in Ben and Jerry's.

If you're curious to know why the above sentence works, look at this beginning:

Profits on imports partly compensate for the current burden on the manufacturing side.

Say what? You'd think because this sentence is short, the chances are pretty good it will also be clear. Not with this writer. Only a Herculean effort or no effort at all could produce such unintelligible prose in so few words.

Here's my favorite business opening. It's from a letter about the McDonald's hamburger chain and its founder, Ray Kroc.

If cows watched horror movies, their favorite monster would be Ray Kroc.

This one's not only short, clear, simple, and somewhat personal, it's vivid, interesting, and funny.

How would you compare these two versions of the same story?

They started walking at dusk, two teenagers casually spreading the message that the streets of West Los Angeles were no longer safe. First they stopped Phillip Lerner and demanded money.

Day by day, America's all too familiar crime clock ticks faster and faster. Every 24 minutes, a murder is committed somewhere in the United States.

They're both good, aren't they? The first, a narrative description of the event, was written for *Newsweek*; the second, a statistical opening, comes from *Time*. But the point is the same: There is no best way to write anything; there is no limit to what we can create. Generally speaking, however, the most effective opening sentences are short, clear, simple, easy to read, vivid, personal, and to the point.

How do you write an opening sentence that's short, clear, simple, easy to read, vivid, personal, and to the point?
Write it last.
If you cluster and then freewrite every message you want to send someone, you'll notice two things: You'll never have trouble getting started, and 40 percent of the time, your opening sentence will be satisfactory. For that other 60 percent, however, wait until *after* you've revised your paragraphs, sentences, phrases, and words. Then go back and rewrite your opening sentence. Having clustered, freewritten, and re-read your memo or letter the four or five times it takes to revise it, you'll be so close to your subject, you should be able to write within two minutes an opening sentence that is short, clear, simple, easy to read, vivid, personal, and to the point.

Proofread Out Loud

Many of the students taking remedial courses in writing centers at the City University of New York have very low reading levels. Some of them can no more understand the concept of a noun or adjective than they can discuss Einstein's theory of relativity. Yet many of these students greatly improve their ability to express themselves on paper by following a two-step approach developed by the writing centers.

The two steps are:

1. *Write as closely as possible to the way you speak.* We speak in simple, clear sentences. Simple, clear sentences are easy to write and easy to punctuate. If we write as closely as possible to the way we speak, we'll reduce the number of grammatical errors we make.

2. *Proofread out loud.* When we proofread, we tend to rely almost exclusively on our eyes. Few of us realize that our ears are also reliable editors. Read out loud what you have written; listen to the way it *sounds*. If it does not sound the way you sound when you speak, change it. The closer you can bring your written prose to your speaking prose, the more authentic and less artificial it will be. Proofreading out loud, as students in the City University of New York writing centers have discovered, *automatically* eliminates 60 percent of your grammatical errors.

THE THOROUGH WAY

"Then you should say what you mean," the March Hare went on.

"I do," Alice hastily replied; "at least—at least I mean what I say—that's the same thing, you know."

"Not the same thing a bit!" said the Hatter. "Why you might just as well say that 'I see what I eat' is the same thing as 'I eat what I see'!"

—*Lewis Carroll*

Rewriting the thorough way takes advantage of the luxury of time. The more time you've created for yourself through clustering and freewriting, the more opportunities you have to make sure what you've written is as close as possible to the way you want it to be.

Do Everything You Did for the Fast Way, Then Type a Fresh Draft

A typed draft not only eliminates the corrections you've already made, it also frees you to focus on the words, sentences, and paragraphs without having to decipher your handwriting. If you use a computer when you write, get a printout. Those individual paragraphs that show up on your terminal screen are excellent for piecemeal editing, but the view is too focused. You need to see your work as a whole now.

Take a Break

After clustering, freewriting, rewriting, and typing, you need one. A long one. Go out to lunch, play a game of tennis, or take a nap. Better yet, if you have the time, go home. Let what you've written sit in a drawer for the night. The more distance you put between you and your writing, the more objective your reading will be.

It also doesn't hurt to take small breaks every fifteen or twenty minutes during the course of your revision. As Yogi Berra would put it, "Just because you ain't working on something doesn't mean you ain't working on it."

Ask Yourself These General Questions About What You've Written

Is It Clear? Does it say what I want to say in a way that is clear, straightforward, easy to read, and easy to understand?

Is It Focused? Does it get to the point? Most of the time, the sooner we make our point, the better.

Is It Efficient? Does it contain any unnecessary words? E. B. White tells us, "A sentence should contain no unnecessary words, a paragraph no unnecessary sentences, for the same reason a drawing should have no unnecessary lines and a machine no unnecessary parts." The more unnecessary words we can strip away, the more energy we'll preserve in our writing.

When we freewrite, we really do come as close as possible to the way we speak. It's only natural to use more words than we need or digress from the point we are trying to make. This is why, when we rewrite, we have to decide *exactly* what we mean and *exactly* how we want to say it.

Finding the critical points in our messages, underlining them, and giving them separate paragraphs of their own can help us help our readers understand us better. So will proofreading out loud. Listen to the places where you stumble over words either because they're too long or have been placed in a confusing sentence. Where do we become distracted or bored? These are the points where we have to get back to the core, to the energy that cutting words preserves.

Because of the way we've been taught to write, however, many people have a difficult time eliminating anything from what they've written. And how could they not? Having invested all that time and energy in every word, they don't want to cut any now. Those words have become valuable signs of the effort they've made.

Those who freewrite, on the other hand, know they're going to edit. By focusing on the process rather than the product, they're not trying to make every word perfect the first time it hits the paper. They know that freewriting demands rewriting, and because freewriting involves relatively little time and energy, they feel less anxious about cutting the fat from their prose.

If, however, you find it hard to elimate words from your freewritten draft, there is one thing you can do to improve your editing efficiency: Practice eliminating with a pen or pencil any unnecessary words you may read in your local newspaper or in the memos and letters you receive. Then, after a few weeks, try to be as ruthless with your own writing as you were with others'.

Is It Concise?   As with so much in life, less in writing is usually more. Also, there's no reason to use big words and big sentences when small words and small sentences will do. Winston Churchill tells us, "Small words are best, and the old small words are best of all." Mark Twain once wrote, "I never use the word 'metropolis' because I'm always paid the same amount of money to write 'city.'"

How much more money do you think writers in the Pentagon earned for writing "wooden interdental stimulators" instead of "toothpicks"? Or, to put it another way, how much did we taxpayers have to shell out for these stimulators?

If you don't work for the Pentagon, try to follow Mark Twain's advice. Abraham Lincoln did. Of the 275 words in his Gettysburg Address, 196 have only one syllable.

Is It Complete? Does it contain all the information the reader needs to know? "Needs" is the important word here. We rarely have to tell our readers everything we know about our subjects, just what they *need* to know.

Is It Positive? Friedrich Nietzsche tells us, "We often dispute an opinion when what we really object to is the tone in which the opinion was uttered." Ask yourself: Is the tone of my voice condescending or patronizing in any way? Are there any words, such as "misinformed," "questionable," or "failure," that might make my reader defensive? Can I present anything negative in a positive light?

Instead of saying, for example, what my company rejects, can I focus on what it accepts or approves of?

Is It Accurate? Have I exaggerated anything, been unfair in any way, and distinguished between what is opinion and what is fact? Have I checked all my facts? Have I used any words that might mislead the reader into thinking something other than what I intended?

Is It Correct? Remember the two-step approach to self-editing taught in writing centers at the City University of New York? (See page 47.) Remember how those students who (1) learned to write in their own voices and (2) proofread out loud automatically eliminated 60 percent of their grammatical errors? How many different kinds of mistakes do you think any one student made after following these two steps?

Three.

Think about that.

Can you imagine students, some with reading levels as low as the third grade, making no more than three kinds of grammatical errors?

Their problem, however—and we share this problem with them—is that each student made his or her particular three mistakes over and over and over again.

So, once you've written as you speak and proofread out loud, how do you discover your three or fewer mistakes and learn to stop repeating them? One way is to establish a formal "buddy system" with someone where you work. Give your letters to this person. Ask him or her to correct maybe five or six letters over the course of several weeks. When you get each corrected letter back, make a list of your mistakes. Add to the list the mistakes from each corrected letter. Only don't just add the new mistakes. List every single mistake every single time. You'll notice that after five or six letters, the same mistakes keep showing up. Those are the two or three mistakes you're most likely to make. Once you've identified them, turn to Chapter 5, "Mechanics," and learn how to correct them for yourself. Then, in future writings, keep a special lookout for the two or three errors you're most likely to make.

Move from the General to the Particular

Having asked these general questions about what we've written, we can take a closer look at our paragraphs, sentences, and words.

The Paragraphs. Count the number of lines in each of your paragraphs and write each number in the margin. If all your numbers are about the same—say, 9, 8, 7, 9, or 3, 5, 4, 4—then all your paragraphs are pretty much the same length and you are unconsciously lulling your reader to sleep. Vary the length of your paragraphs. Make some nine lines long, some four, some even one sentence or one word long.

Contrary to what we were taught in grammar school, paragraphs don't have to have a beginning, middle, and end. They can be as short as one sentence or even one word. One-word paragraphs are pretty powerful paragraphs. Instead of thinking of paragraphs as having a beginning, middle, and end, you may wish to consider their having these three elements:

UNITY. Have I assigned basically one idea to each paragraph?

COHERENCE. Does each sentence within the paragraph flow logically into the next?

EMPHASIS. Have I placed the important information at the beginning and end of each paragraph?

The Sentences. Draw a slash through each period. If the distance between the slashes is pretty much the same, all your sentences are pretty much the same length, and if all your sentences are the same length, you're putting the reader to sleep. So vary the length of your sentences. And try to keep them alive. Don't start off slow, sag in the middle, or trail off at the end.

Sentences that begin with the words "There is . . ." or "There are . . . ," for example, usually start off slow. Not that there is anything wrong with this. *There are* many times when we want to begin a sentence with "There is . . ." or "There are . . ." The trouble is we begin too many sentences this way. Whatever power these words may have had has been lost.

The same goes for sentences beginning with "It . . ." As in "It appears . . ." and "It has been recently brought to my attention that . . ." *There is* nothing wrong with beginning our sentences this way. *It* is just that we do it too often.

Another way to move our sentences along is by placing our supporting ideas *after* rather than *before* our main ideas. For example, "As a result of the increase in membership, your dues are going down" might be more engaging if it were written, "Your dues are going down because our membership has gone up."

As with sentences beginning with "There is . . ." or "It . . . ," there is nothing wrong with using a long, formal-sounding clause to introduce the main idea of your sentence. You just want to avoid doing it too often.

Even good things can be overdone. Take, for example, the maxim that short sentences are more effective than long sentences. Generally speaking, they are, but too many short sentences in a row can be as devastating as an introductory clause that doesn't know when to end.

Consider this letter from a small publishing house in Oregon:

We received your order for a copy of Bruce Forer's *Why We Write*. Unfortunately, the book isn't ready yet. A breakdown in our printing department has caused a delay. We have since installed new machines. They will be in operation soon. Please accept our apologies for the delay. Thank you for being patient.

And not just for the books! Any two or three of these sentences in a row would give pause to no one, but seven in a row is almost more than any reader can stand.

The Phrases. Having eliminated as best we can whatever clichés, jargon, or bureaucratic phrases that have slipped into our writing, we may want to look at our prepositions. We tend to make a parade of them whenever we try to say too much in one sentence.

Journalists are to blame for this. Trained to get the who, what, why, when, and where for every story they write, they've also been trained to put that who, what, why, when, and where in the first sentence of whatever they write. The result is often something like this: "Michael Harrington, 38, *of* 24 High Street *in* Birmingham was shot yesterday as he drove his car *over* the section *of* I–65 currently *under* construction."

Too many prepositional phrases in a row drains the reader's energy. Unless you're an excellent writer or writing so close to the way you speak that no one notices, three consecutive prepositional phrases is just about as many as most people can read without becoming irritated. Four in a row is almost certainly a disaster. If you have four or more consecutive prepositional phrases, see if you can't spread the information they contain over several sentences. Or perhaps some of it can be placed in another paragraph.

The Words. When we proofread what we write, we tend to look mostly at the nouns. Because they name people, places, and things, we think they are the most important words. In many cases, they are, but in terms of the writing, the most important words are the verbs.

Verbs are where the action is. And the best verbs rarely need an adverb. In fact, you can use any adverbs you've written as indicating a need for more powerful verbs.

Of all the verbs available to us, only two kinds need to be looked at twice: verbs written in the passive voice and forms of the verb "to be."

ACTIVE VOICE VS. PASSIVE VOICE. Active voice is when the subject of a sentence does the action: John hit the ball. "John" is the subject; "John" is doing the action. Passive voice is when the action is being done to the subject: The ball was hit by John. "Ball" is the subject; the action is being done by "John."

As with so much of what we've said about fine-tuning our prose, there is nothing wrong with writing in the passive voice. If we're trying to downplay something, for example, or avoid some responsibility, the passive voice is the way to do it. Generally speaking, however, sentences written in the active voice are cleaner, clearer, shorter, and more engaging for the reader.

FORMS OF THE VERB "TO BE." There's nothing wrong with any of these forms; they've just lost some of their power from being overused. If you've written four or five sentences in a row and all your verbs are linked with one or any of these six words—*am, is, are, was, were, been*—see if you can replace a few of these forms with other verbs. A sentence such as "He is going to be here on Tuesday," for example, could be changed to "He arrives on Tuesday" if the sentences before and after it also feature forms of the verb "to be."

A second kind of word to take a closer look at is the adjective. Using the first adjectives that come to mind when we freewrite is a good way to get started and to keep going. But for the final draft, see if you can replace some of those adjectives with more specific details. This will help you write more effectively about what you want to say and plant longer-lasting images in your readers' minds.

When you've finished typing your working draft, circle any adjectives you come across as you proofread. For each adjective, ask yourself, "What do I mean by this word?" Then replace the adjective with your answer. Or, if you like the adjective you've chosen, keep it, and then say in the next sentence what you mean by it. The more specific the details about what you're describing, the sharper your reader's focus.

Remember Charlotte's story about her horrible boss Tommy Snipe? What's the first thing to come into your mind? The fish going down the toilet, right? What's the next thing you remember? The recycled card? The leather gloves costing half a week's salary? The dirty clothes Snipe tosses on Charlotte's desk? What we remember most are the specific details Charlotte uses to describe her boss. She also uses a lot of adjectives—"fat," "short," "pompous," "ill-mannered," and more—but the only description we're likely to recall is the one that left a specific image in our minds, without an adjective: Snipe smelled like his cigar. Without specific, concrete details, our writing becomes totally mental. And it doesn't matter whether we're writing about a person, place, product, service, or idea: Details make the difference.

Know When to Quit

Yes, it is possible to overwrite, to correct so many things you squeeze the life out of what you've written. Keep the larger purpose in mind: good, interesting, imaginative prose.

One way to keep your writing from becoming perfunctory or boring is to worry less. As you develop through clustering and freewriting your ability to put words on paper, you'll find yourself naturally developing the kind of critical consciousness that makes writing good, easy, and effective. In other words, do the best you can in the time you have available. Then let it go.

HOW TO EDIT OTHERS

> The main responsibility of editors is not only to exceed their best standards but to value good writing by insisting on quality. Get into a teaching relationship with your writers. Look for people who care about words. Care about words yourself.
>
> —*William Zinsser*

Although this book is primarily concerned with our own writing, we are often put in the position of having to edit other people's writing. When you are in that position, perhaps the most important thing to remember is this: Editing is not autopsy. We do not always have to find something wrong with every piece of writing we're asked to work on. Nor, if we can't find anything wrong, do we have to make changes to justify our paychecks. That kind of approach may enlarge the ego, but it shrinks the soul.

The relationship between editor and writers may be inherently antagonistic, but we editors know where the power lies. It is with us, the ones with the last word. We also carry the final responsibility for what is written, however. We're on the line too, even if our names don't appear anywhere.

Perhaps for this reason, we tend to be more conservative than writers, more left brained than right, more concerned with being correct than interesting. This is as it should be. But we also have a responsibility to help our writers say what *they* want to say, even if we would say it differently. Our job is not to tear apart the work we've been given but to put it together. When we do have to cut, we do it with the scalpel, not the cleaver.

There are three steps every good editor follows: Read, examine, listen. And as with prewriting, freewriting, and rewriting, these steps are not performed simultaneously.

Read

The worst editors are those who begin reading with pens in their hands. They're ready to make corrections before they've even found out what their writers are trying to say. And once they make their first correction, there's no stopping them. Everything from that point on is edited to confirm the original change.

Editors! Read what you've been given all the way to the end before making any changes. Find out what the writer wants to say, not what you would say if you were in the writer's place. To do this, you may have to sit on your hands for a few minutes while you read or perhaps go into a room where there are no pens or terminals, but you must not make a mark anywhere until you've read the whole memo, letter, report, or story. Then, if you still don't understand what you've read, give it back to the writer. Say you are confused, ask the writer what he or she had in mind, allow the writer to clear up anything that is unclear or inconcise or incoherent. The importance of understanding what the writer was trying to say and letting the writer correct his or own shortcomings cannot be overemphasized. This not only preserves the writer's ego—and writers know they have to invest their egos in their writing if they want to make it good—it shows the writer whose side you're on. Trust, confidence, and a willingness to listen to suggestions or even accept changes soon follow.

Examine

"Examine" does not mean "change." It means to study, weigh, consider, and analyze. In examining the writer's work, move from the general to the particular.

Is It Architecturally Sound? Does the beginning grab our attention? Does what follows keep it? Are there clues of what to expect as we move along? This doesn't mean there are no surprises, but that any surprises can be quickly understood and appreciated.

And what about the end? Is it strong or weak? Has the writer saved something good for last, or does the writing just peter out as if the writer has run out of things to say?

Does It Flow? Is the writing easy to read even if the subject is complex? Does any information get in the way of our understanding? Might some of it be left out? Or presented in a graph?

Are there dull phrases or unnecessary words? Can "at this point in time," for example, be changed to "now" or "then"? Can "because" substitute for "due to the fact that"? Until an "actual experience" becomes an "experience," a room is "filled to capacity" instead of just "filled," and we no longer "ask the question" but merely "ask," there will be much to eliminate. Fortunately, this is one area where editors are sure to win praise with writers and readers.

Is It Mechanically Sound? In spite of what many writers think, grammar is not an arbitrary set of rules designed to make their lives more difficult. And editors who believe grammar has only to do with being correct also miss the point. According to this view, the rules of grammar help writers demonstrate their mastery of the language. But the rules of grammar also have a rhetorical purpose: to help writers communicate their ideas and make it easier for readers to understand them.

For this reason, the first question we editors want to ask is not whether an unfamiliar sentence structure or particular use of a punctuation mark is right or wrong but does it work. For example, "does it work" in the previous sentence is a question. Shouldn't it end with a question mark? But what would be the effect if it did? Wouldn't that make the whole sentence a question, when it isn't? Which, then, is "correct"? The answer is: the one that works best. If the sentence ending with "does it work" came at the end of a long argument by an exasperated writer, an exclamation point (!) might work best.

When it comes to grammar, it's important for us to realize that the language made the rules, not the other way around. And when it comes to editing, we should try to remember the importance and relevance of content and context.

Does the Lead Lead?   Does the opening sentence grab our readers' attention and point them in the direction we want them to go? Is it limited to one or two ideas? Is it short but not so short as to leave out information the reader may deserve? Is it as bold and as forceful as the subject will allow?

Is the Writing Generally Sound?   Give what you've edited one final read. Again, do it without your pen. If the piece holds together in a sound and worthy way, make an appointment with the writer.

Listen

Of the three steps in the editing process—read, examine, and listen—the last is the most important for developing a compatible relationship between editor and writer. If this one doesn't work, the first two will also fail.

The first response of an editor to a writer should be that of a person, not a professional. Say how you feel about the writer's ideas, thoughts, opinions, and insights. Show you care. Share with the writer any similar experiences you may have had. In short, be a human being. Try to break down any barriers that may exist between you in your roles as writer and editor.

Then listen. It's so easy in conferences with writers for editors to do most of the talking. Somehow we feel it's our job to tell the writer what's wrong with his or her writing, and it's up to the writer to make sure the same "mistakes" never reappear, even though we know full well that much of what we call "error" has more to do with fashion and some of what we would "correct," dozens of other editors would find "correct" as is.

Try, then, not to "correct." In fact, the less talking we do, the better. Let the writers ask what they need to learn. If they don't know, don't tell them. Help them discover it by asking questions that will lead them to it. For example, you might ask:

- What did you learn from this piece of writing?
- Do you have any plans for a next draft?
- Was there anything about your writing that surprised you?
- Based on this piece of writing, where do you think you are heading as a writer?
- What do you like about what you've written?
- Do you have any questions you'd like to ask me?

These questions were developed by Donald Murray, an editor, teacher, and Pulitzer Prize-winning writer. Murray also suggests that, if you do have something to say to the writer, you speak about it in terms of the writer's immediate needs. Try to be as specific as you can by avoiding rhetorical principles and editing jargon. "This isn't clear" doesn't mean anything to a writer if you can't say what it is, specifically, that confuses you.

Also, "This isn't clear" is negative. Couldn't we just as easily say, "How can we show our readers why it's important for them to act now?" Some editors avoid the words "good" and "bad" or "right" and "wrong" altogether. They've found writers respond better to words like "more effective" and "less effective."

Murray has some other suggestions for improving the relationship between editors and writers. In a book called *How I Wrote the Story*, Murray asked the writers and editors at the *Providence Journal* to list ways they help or hinder one another. Behind a shield of anonymity, they came up with over 100 ways.

Here are some of the ways an editor can help a writer:

CONFER. Decide together what you want and don't want. Give reasons.

LISTEN. Don't judge in advance what the writer should produce. Open your mind and be willing to admit you might learn something.

SUPPORT. Not with phony pats on the back but with genuine compliments and useful criticism.

CHALLENGE. Encourage unconventional techniques, question the writer's assumptions, offer a different view, and make suggestions without insisting they be used.

REMEMBER. Psychologically bad editing is far more damaging than technically bad editing. An editing mistake can be forgotten in a week; a mistake in how you treat the writer can be remembered for a lifetime.

Here are some of the ways a writer can help an editor:

CONFER. Ask for advice, tell the editor why you did what you did, be open to suggestions, be willing to take criticism, talk before writing if you can, and keep a flow of ideas going. Don't just wait for the editor's ideas.

LISTEN. Don't resist reasonable suggestions; you don't know it all yet. On the other hand, don't bend when the bending isn't justified. Sometimes editors need to be told when a change shouldn't be made.

SUPPORT. Editors need all the help they can get. Meet your deadlines, proofread your work, don't take criticism personally, use your dictionary every once in a while, be thorough and accurate about your facts, and try to understand that editors have schedules too.

CHALLENGE. Editors need feedback. Question their preconceived notions about what constitutes good writing, but do it gently. Believe it or not, editors are even more insecure than writers.

REMEMBER. Editors are people too. Try not to always refer to them as "butchers." They need to be stroked just as much as writers.

CONCLUSION

Rewriting is called rewriting because we do it *after* we've already written something. Nevertheless, most of us have a difficult time trying not to rewrite *while* we write. We think we're going to forget the change we have in mind or, if we correct something now, we won't have to correct it later. What we don't realize is that trying to write and rewrite simultaneously is like building with one hand while destroying with the other. For one thing, it puts pressure on us. It makes our success depend on everything running smoothly. What happens when we're out of practice? Or not feeling well? Or lacking confidence? Or the phone won't stop ringing? Or we change our mind halfway through whatever it is we're writing?

Getting it right the first time is also a waste of time. You have to figure out in your mind what you want to say before you can say it. Then you have to make sure it all comes out right on the paper, which means writing slowly and carefully. You find yourself pausing between sentences to make sure you're still going in the right direction. This often leads to overwriting, putting in too many details. It also keeps you from exploring other possibilities. Locked into a predetermined mind-set, your best thinking is shut off before you even begin.

So why not let yourself write it wrong the first time? Or even a second or third time? Not only is it still faster and easier than writing it right the first time, you'll discover more about your subject and yourself. And when you finish writing, you won't feel bad about cutting any of it because there'll be more to cut and you won't have invested so much time and energy in it.

This last point cannot be overemphasized. Cutting is the key to successful revision. In *Write with Power*, Peter Elbow says that to be good rewriters, we have to learn the pleasure of the knife, to distance ourselves from our work, and, with a certain ruthlessness, get rid of anything that's bad, inappropriate, or unnecessary.

If you find this difficult, Elbow suggests you look at cutting as painful only when it's done in a fruitless way. Try to look *through* your words to what they *could* be. Try practicing on other people's work first. Use a red pen if you really want to get into it. Not only will you develop effective rewriting techniques sooner, you'll also learn to enjoy the experience of changing things that don't work. When that time comes, says Elbow, you're ready to turn your scalpel on yourself.

—4—

$\int$TYLE

DEVELOPING ONE OF YOUR OWN

THE POOR WRITER'S ALMANACK

Initially, God created the heaven and the earth.
Do it presently!
Seek and ye shall locate.
Come and obtain it!
God assists those whose assist themselves.
Man is born unto inconvenience, as the sparks fly
    upward.
In the event that initially you fail to succeed,
    endeavor, endeavor, endeavor again.
A rose by any other designation would smell as
    sweet.
Residence, sweet residence.
And they lived happily ever subsequently.
Furnish us this day our daily bread.
All's well that terminates well.
Sufficient and to spare.
Deceased as a doornail.

—Rudolf Flesch

Your style is the way you say and do things. It's what makes
you who you are, what separates you from everyone else,
what identifies you as you. In the same way that you have
your own particular ways of speaking and acting, you also
have your own particular ways of writing. Or rather, you
should have.

65

Unfortunately, most of us don't know what our writing style is because we never had an opportunity to discover and develop one. Instead, we were taught to adopt other people's styles. The effect is not much different from what happens when you adopt another person's hair-do. It may be all right in and of itself, but it just doesn't look right on you. It just doesn't fit your personality.

I have an uncle. He's president of an insurance company in Philadelphia. He's also from Brooklyn, New York. Like a lot of people from Brooklyn, he has highly developed verbal skills. He got them from hanging out on the street talking with the other kids on the block.

My uncle also has a good sense of humor. People love to be around him because he's so funny. As my friend Bruce once said of him, "Your uncle always rises to the verbal occasion, and he almost always does it through humor."

Let me give you an example. Several years ago, I was living in California. My uncle was visiting me. He was on the balcony of my apartment, while I was reading in the living room. Suddenly, he called out to me, "Richit! Richit!"—my uncle still has his Brooklyn accent—"Come out here! Des boids everywhere. Beeyootifull boids. Like we never had in Brooklyn."

I bounded out onto the balcony, and sure enough, they *were* beautiful. Like nothing we ever saw in Brooklyn. Feathers everywhere. But I enjoy teasing my uncle about his insecurities, so I said, "Dick, they're lovely, but I have to tell you something. Out here in California? They're not 'boids'; they're 'birds.' "

Dick thought about this for a minute. Then he said, "But Richit. They choiped like boids."

That way of talking, that quick sense of humor is my uncle. No one else can be him the way he can, and people love him for the way that he is. That way that separates him from everyone else is his *style*.

But that endearing, engaging style is rarely present when

Dick writes a letter. Then it's all "Pursuant to our conversation . . ." and "Enclosed herewith please find . . . ." One time, in a letter to me, his nephew, Dick referred to himself as "the undersigned." When I wrote back, I referred to him as "the abovementioned."

He didn't even notice.

Look at this memo from Tom Watson, a past chairman of the executive committee at International Business Machines:

TO ALL IBM MANAGERS:

A foreign language has been creeping into many of the presentations I hear and the memos I read. It adds nothing to a message but noise, and I want your help in stamping it out. It's called gobbledygook.

There's no shortage of examples. Nothing seems to get finished anymore—it gets "finalized." Things don't happen at the same time but "coincident with this action." Believe it or not, people will talk about taking a "commitment position" and then because of the "volatility of schedule changes" they will "decommit" so that our "posture vis-à-vis some data base that needs a sizing will be able to enhance competitive positions."

That's gobbledygook.

It may be acceptable among bureaucrats but not in this company. IBM wasn't built with fuzzy ideas and pretentious language. IBM was built with clear thinking and plain talk. Let's keep it that way.

Compare Watson's message with this paragraph for workers in the California Consumer Affairs Department:

TENSES, GENDER, AND NUMBER

For the purpose of clarifying the rules and regulations contained in this chapter, the present tense includes the past and future tenses, and the future the present; the

masculine gender includes the feminine and the feminine
the masculine; and the singular includes the plural and
the plural the singular.

The fastest, easiest, most effective way to avoid this kind
of writing and develop the kind of powerful, lively, engaging style that characterizes Watson's memo is to write
as closely as possible to the way we speak, in what a writer
calls "my own voice."

To do this we have to write almost the exact opposite of
the way we were taught. Instead of learning to discover
and develop our own natural writing voices, we learned to
model other people's voices. Our first models were those
boring sentences from which we had to pick out all the
nouns. Other models included poems, short stories, and
novels that were written by writers our teachers told us
were "good." We were expected to write like these people,
to imitate their styles. Our teachers called these styles "standards." To give good grades to a student who couldn't write
like one of the models was to lower these standards.

The problem with these model writers was that, as good
as they were, they didn't sound like us. But because we
were told that their way was the "correct" way to write, and
because we were too young to know any better, and because
we trusted our teachers to have all the "right" answers, we
tried really hard to fit our writing into the molds that had
been created for us. Rarely did we do any creating of our
own. Or if we did, only that which coincided with our
teachers' preconceived ideas about what constituted good
writing was acceptable. Everything else was "improper."

Two things came from this: We were corrected every
time we failed to write "proper English," and whatever
confidence we might have developed in our writing ability
was undermined by the false models we were taught to
imitate. No one ever told us that those great writers didn't
get to be great writers by listening to what their teachers

told them. They discovered they had to find their own ways of writing, their own individual voices, the ones that separated them from all the other writers.

No one ever told us that! We were taught to follow the rules even though many of our model writers didn't. When we pointed this out to our teachers, however, we were told these writers had a "poetic license." They could do whatever they wanted with the language. When we became famous, we could have a poetic license too. In the meantime, we'd do what we were told, which in our minds meant setting aside the Billy Smith or Debbie Duncan who played games everyday and becoming William P. Smith or D. B. Duncan every time we picked up a pen.

Fortunately, we now know this isn't the most effective way to learn to write. Enough "good" writers have told us how they had to spend a great part of their careers unlearning all their teachers taught them about what characterized good writing. These writers learned that to become "good" they had to discover and develop their own natural writing voices.

Now this doesn't mean they learned to write *exactly* as they talked. That would cause only chaos. They learned to express themselves in a way that sounded natural and effortless but had been edited for clarity and conciseness.

We have many different speaking voices. Altogether, these voices make up our speaking style. A lot of little styles add up to one big one, if you will. Which particular voice we use depends on whom we are speaking to. We speak one way to our children and another way to our parents. The voice we use with our friends differs from the one our colleagues hear. And our bosses probably hear a different voice than the people we supervise.

Our first job as writers, then, is to find our own natural writing voices. Freewriting (see pages 27–39) is the best place to start because it really is as close as possible to the ways we speak. Once we have *our* words on paper, we can edit them to fit the standard level of English our readers expect our writing to have. In other words, freewriting helps us to develop a style that still reflects our characters and personalities.

To become polished writers, however, we need to develop confidence in ourselves as people. We can't accept, for example, that we have nothing interesting to say or no interesting ways of saying it. Our experiences and our voices, like the experiences and voices of all good writers, are unique. So are our thoughts and feelings. The trick is to make whatever subject we have to write about our own. Make what we write as true to the way we see things as we can. And care about it. Most readers know when we're saying what we think we ought to or trying to be something we're not. If you're a Bill Smith or a Deborah Duncan, Bill Smith or Deborah Duncan is who your readers want to hear from. The minute you become a William P. Smith or a D. B. Duncan, your investment in your writing and your concern about what you write will diminish. And so will your reader's investment and concern.

Now this doesn't mean that the rules we learned about writing aren't important. Just that they shouldn't get in the way. For example, do you remember being told that good writers don't repeat words? Imagine if Abraham Lincoln believed this and had written "of the people, by the persons, and for all the men, women, and children" instead of "of the people, by the people, and for the people." Imagine Winston Churchill telling us to "fight on the beaches, battle on the landing grounds, wages war in the fields and in the streets, engage the enemy in the hills, and never surrender." Churchill repeated not one word, he repeated three: "We shall fight on the beaches, we shall fight on the landing grounds, we shall fight in the fields and in the streets, we shall fight in the hills; we shall never surrender."

How about the rule never to end a sentence in a preposition? Remember that one? Thanks to Winston Churchill, it's okay now to end our sentences in prepositions. Churchill made us realize the absurdity of this rule when, speaking ironically, he said, "This is the type of arrant pedantry up with which I will not put." If we end our sentences in prepositions when we speak, we can also end them with prepositions when we write.

We've also been told to *never* split our infinitives, but if you're going to split one, isn't putting the absolute "never" between "to" and "split" a good way to do it?

Even the suggestions you read in this book don't apply to every situation. In an earlier chapter, for example, you were warned about the prepositional parade: "Too many prepositional phrases in a row drain the reader's energy. Three consecutive prepositional phrases is just about as many as most people can handle. Four in a row is almost certainly a disaster." The truth of this statement is easy to recognize in a kiss-of-death sentence like "The Danubian basin . . . is a relatively closed geographical unit which began to change rapidly . . . *under* the impact *of* forces *at* work *within* the core area *of* the rising global economic system." But is our prepositional parade offensive in this sentence: "Please come to the rear of the school for your chldren at the end of the day"? Both sentences contain five prepositional phrases in a row. The first we can't stand, but the second is tolerable because it is so close to the way we speak.

To try to improve your writing by increasing your knowledge of the rules; otherwise, substituting new rules for old ones isn't going to help much. There's a big difference between writing "correctly" and writing well. Rules are effective only insofar as they help us make our messages clear. They are only a means, not an end.

The best way to make the rules work for you is to be motivated. Have something to say and want to say it. If the writing isn't inspired, the reading won't be either. If, on the other hand, you care about what you say and how your reader perceives you, you will probably write well and look for whatever other tools you need to write better.

This attitude toward our subjects cannot be overemphasized. It determines our style. If we're angry about something, our style is going to reflect that anger. And there's nothing wrong with being angry, but what if our anger works against us without our realizing it? What if our attitude toward a subject is not the most effective way to reach our readers? Even a well-intentioned message, if inappropriate, can be devastating.

In his book *Prose Style,* Wilfred Stone tells the story of a telegram sent to a union official who had suffered a heart attack. The telegram read: "The board of Local 1245 last night passed a resolution wishing you a speedy recovery by a vote of 18 to 17." Obviously the writer was looking for a light touch, something to bring a smile to the union official's face. For reasons equally obvious, he failed.

Most errors in attitude, however, are not accidental. As Stone points out, they usually reflect a deep misreading of the writer's subject, the audience, or both. And it usually doesn't do much good to try to hide these attitudes. Our readers are experts at picking out phoniness. In fact, our readers are sometimes better at identifying our real attitudes toward certain subjects than we are.

According to Stone, there are three kinds of attitudes we want to avoid: the pompous, the highbrow, and the flippant.

The Pompous. Pomposity is the unwillingness to communicate in a simple, straightforward way. It is the language of computers, bureaucrats, and functionaries, not people.

My favorite example of pompous writing comes from George Orwell. To demonstrate how effectively the pompous style separates us from our audience, Orwell took a quotation from Ecclesiastes:

> I returned and saw under the sun, that the race is not
> to the swift, nor the battle to the strong, neither yet bread

to the wise, nor yet riches to men of understanding; but time and chance happeneth to them all.

Then he translated it into the kind of pompous language we've all become so familiar with:

Objective consideration of contemporary phenomena compels the conclusion that success or failure in competitive activities exhibits no tendency to be commensurate with innate capacity, but that a considerable element of the unpredictable must invariably be taken into account.

There are some big words here. No doubt a ponderous mind is at work. But would you want to have lunch with this person?

The Highbrow. Highbrow writing is similar to pompous writing in the sense that it stems from a lack of confidence in the writer. Rather than mask the writer's insecurity, however, it reveals it. The difference in highbrow writing is that it is usually deliberate. Whereas pompous writers lead themselves to false notions of their own dignity and the dignity of their writing, highbrow writers want to show off. Highbrow writers want us all to be aware of what we don't know.

Writing the program notes for a concert at the Tanglewood Music Festival, Steven Ledbetter explains the first movement in a Beethoven quartet:

The beginning, with unaccompanied violin outlining a seventh and waiting, poised, for the others to produce a chord against which it might settle downward, is utterly unique. The transition lands suddenly in a very foreign key, but Beethoven hurries out of it to the expected secondary key of A major and brings the exposition to an end with a dramatic, chromatic cello part climbing in half-steps from A to C-sharp, which harmonizes both the repeat of the exposition (the first time) and the beginning of the development (the second time).

If only there were space in the program guide to drop a few names, Ledbetter's self-advertisement would be complete. Out to *im*press rather than *ex*press, he widens, rather than narrows, the distance between him and his readers—if he has any. Instead of leading better, as his name implies, he leads us worse than not at all.

The Flippant. The flippant writer offends by not taking seriously a subject the reader may feel is important. The person who sent that telegram to the union official with the heart attack was being flippant. He didn't mean any harm and can easily be forgiven, but his message wasn't appreciated.

A good example of how damaging flippancy can be is seen in the career of Gore Vidal. A first-rate mind, an insightful historian, and a talented novelist, Vidal has had his political aspirations continually undermined by his caustic wit. Yet after all these years and two failed campaigns for office, he still hasn't made the connection. When recently asked, for instance, which social class he belonged to, Vidal said he was a third-generation celebrity, that he belonged to the celebrity class, the greatest class of all. He was being flippant, but many people took him literally and wrote him off as a snob. Others become confused. And Vidal didn't help. He is often flippant about the Kennedys for example, but serious about taxing churches and restructuring the U.S. Constitution along British lines. When he argues to legalize all drugs and any kind of sex between consenting adults, many people can't tell whether he is flippant or serious. Some think both.

These attitudes that we have toward our subjects and

readers determine our style. And we have as many styles as we do attitudes. The trick is to adapt these attitudes to the needs and sensibilities of our readers. The way to do this is through respect: respect for our subjects and respect for our readers. "Listen, you creep" is one kind of style reflecting one kind of attitude; "May I be of any help" is another. As Wilfred Stone tells us:

> No matter how sure we are of our opinions, it is elementary courtesy and good sense to acknowledge the reader's existence, the possibility of his disagreement, the potential value of his criticism. No matter how indifferent we may be to our readers, it is elementary courtesy to put them at their ease. Unless we are bent on mayhem, it is elementary good sense to establish a basis of mutual respect.

Did you notice how many times Stone used the word "elementary"?

Is Stone a good or bad writer?

Does calling attention to his use of "elementary" take away from the impact of the quotation?

Because the use of repetition is not a major point in this chapter, could my mentioning it after Stone's important remarks be considered flippant?

Was it wise to want to end this introduction to Chapter 4 with a quotation in the first place? Isn't that one of the "rules"? That we can begin with quotations but not end with them?

These are all questions of style. None of them requires a right or wrong answer. Only an answer to the question, What works best? In this case, should I end with Stone's plea for mutual respect or the point about repetition? The answer is obvious, isn't it.

Now why doesn't that last sentence end with a question mark? It's a question, isn't it? Yes, but isn't it more of a statement? And isn't the writer's attitude reflected better in the statement than the question? And isn't it also a "rule" not to end any piece of writing with a question? Does this rule not to end anything with a question conflict with the rule that all questions should end with a question mark? Which rule should be followed? Which one broken?

The list of questions is as long and as varied as the number of attitudes we hold and the number of styles we use to express these attitudes. Maybe even longer. And few of them can provide us with a "correct" answer. Only the same question: What works best?

PARAGRAPHS

> When I see a paragraph shrinking under my eyes like a strip of bacon in a skillet, I know I'm on the right track.
>
> —*Peter DeVries*

Paragraphs are like rest areas. Without them our eyes and brains would tire quickly. We wouldn't be able to read and absorb as much as we do. Thanks to paragraphs, we know when something is complete. We know that we've come to the end of a group of statements and can rest a moment before going on to the next.

How we divide our messages into paragraphs depends on what we have to say. The content of what we write determines the shape of its container as much as milk or plutonium or any other material. In other words, there are no rules for identifying or developing paragraphs. There are, however, some guidelines.

The guidelines for writing effective paragraphs are often determined by fashion. At the beginning of this century, long paragraphs were the fashion. The reason, according to Vincent Ruggiero in *The Art of Writing,* was the pace of life. There were no radios, televisions, computers, or satellites to speed communication. In the same way that people prepared to spend a long time traveling what today may seem like a short distance, so too were they content to take their time reading. Long paragraphs didn't threaten them because they weren't in as much of a hurry to finish. They could sit back, relax, and enjoy the pleasure of absorbing what they read. Speedreading, as Ruggiero points out, wasn't invented until people needed it.

Today's writers know that, using long paragraphs, they may seem to be taking too much time to say what needs to be said. Today's writers know that long paragraphs discourage people from reading, or if they must read the material, they skip sentences in the middle and hope that the major points will be summarized at the end.

So should all our paragraphs be short? Say, less than five or seven lines? No. And for the same reason that they shouldn't be five or seven pages long. Paragraphs are more than just landmarks for the eyes and brain. They are basic units of thought and feeling. They take what is complex for ourselves and others and organize it into small parts that we can handle one at a time. These smaller parts build one upon the other until an understanding of the larger whole is reached.

Paragraphs, then, must be as long or as short as their subjects require. In many cases, our readers must be given reasons if we are to persuade them to our point of view. They need the details to see what we see. Just to say something is good doesn't work; we have to explain why. On the other hand, too many details drain the power from our messages. The key to details is to give reasons but not every reason we can think of. Only as many as we need to make our point. Too many reasons can bore our readers or make them feel bullied.

How can we determine the too much from the too little? First, by clustering (see pages 14–26) everything we can think of to say about our subjects and eliminating whatever our readers don't need to know. Then by freewriting (see pages 27–39) from one cluster to the next. Because free-writing enables us to say whatever we want to say about a subject however we want to say it, we are given another opportunity to cut anything that isn't absolutely essential.

Clustering and freewriting also help us determine the natural junctures at which to divide our paragraphs. If, however, we are confused as to whether one paragraph might be more effective if divided into two or two paragraphs should be combined into one, we may want to take a look at the specific action we are taking with regard to the subject we are writing about. For example, we may wish to end a paragraph when we finish describing our subject and begin a new paragraph with our analysis of the description. Or we may want to end our analysis and begin a new paragraph with a comparison. Or end on a comparison and begin with an explanation. The list is as long as the ways we have of speaking about our subjects. The important thing is that those times when we give our readers a rest before asking them to continue should at least seem natural. There are few things more irritating to a reader than looking at a page that appeals to the eye but soon reveals combinations of things that should be separated or the forced interruption of things that naturally go together. In other words, our paragraphs should be long enough to convey one thought but never so long as to confuse.

More important than length, however, are the three principles mentioned in the chapter on rewriting (see page 52): (1) unity (basically one idea to each paragraph), (2) coherence (leading the reader from one point to the next), and (3) emphasis (putting the most important information at the beginning and end of each paragraph).

Let's elaborate on these principles:

Unity. Effective writers try to limit each paragraph to a single idea, and this idea is usually stated in the opening sentence. This opening sentence announces the subject of the paragraph and the attitude we want our readers to have toward it. The rest of the sentences in the paragraph explain, elaborate, give examples, or make analyses that support the opening sentence. The closing sentence of each paragraph draws all we've said about the main idea to a conclusion that leads the reader to the next paragraph.

Coherence. Does each sentence flow logically into the next and at the same time connect with all the other sentences in such a way as to make a whole unit of thought or feeling? You can answer this question by writing down in one sentence what each paragraph means. If each of the sentences you've written down doesn't convey the basic logic of what you want to say, you may have gaps in that logical process, you may have included something irrelevant, or you may be guilty of padding your main idea with information that isn't essential. In other words, there must be a sense of purpose and clarity to whatever we put into our paragraphs. We can't say, for example, "Oh, by the way, I meant to tell you . . . ." For our final drafts, we must move from beginning to end, from early to late, from the periphery to the center, from the general to the particular, from the personal to the universal, or whatever other ways our subjects may dictate. Rarely, unless we want to create some kind of realistic or novelistic effect, do we want to scatter the sequence of what we wish to say.

Emphasis. The opening and closing sentences are the best places for throwing our strongest rhetorical punches.

The Opening Sentence

Let's talk about the opening sentences first. They set the tone of what's to follow and establish what the reader can expect from us, but they must do these things in such a way as to grab our readers' attention and make them want to read on.

In Chapter 3, "Rewriting" (see pages 40–64), we discussed the fastest, easiest, and most effective way to write short, simple, clear, engaging, vivid, personal, imaginative, attention-grabbing opening sentences: Write them last. But here are several kinds of opening sentences you may wish to consider for opening your paragraphs.

An Opening Sentence That Gets Right to the Point. We're all familiar with the opening to Abraham Lincoln's Gettysburg Address: "Four score and seven years ago, our fathers brought forth on this continent a new nation conceived in liberty and dedicated to the proposition that all men are created equal." But this, according to Oliver Jensen, is what the Gettysburg Address would sound like if it had been written by Dwight David Eisenhower: "I haven't checked these figures but around 87 years ago, I think it was, a number of individuals organized a governmental set-up here in this country, I believe it concerned the Eastern areas, with this idea they were following up based on a sort of national independence arrangement and the program that every individual is just as good as every other individual."

Jensen's parody doesn't tell us anything more than Lincoln's original, but it takes so long for "Eisenhower" to make his point, he dilutes his impact. We don't get the feeling that "Eisenhower" cares, so why should we?

An Opening Sentence That Asks a Question. "Why should we be in such desperate haste to succeed in such desperate enterprises?" Henry David Thoreau asks us in *Walden*. "If a man does not keep pace with his companions, perhaps it is because he hears a different drummer. Let him step to the music which he hears, however measured or far away."

Or how about this opening to an essay on children who become confused when their divorced parents start dating other people: "It's ten o'clock. Do you know where your Mom is?"

The advantage of an opening sentence that asks a question is that the reader is immediately participating in your subject. That's a big advantage.

An Opening Sentence That Presents a Gripping Fact. "You have a better chance of getting mugged in New York City than you have of winning the state's lottery." That's a gripping way to present a statistic. Compare it with this one on a similar but more terrifying subject: "Last year, more than 2,000 people were murdered in New York."

Don't just state facts. Try to present them in a way that is going to have an impact on the reader. Make them mean something beyond themselves.

An Opening Sentence That Tells the Good News. "You've just been promoted" or "You'll be taking home more money next week" or "Get ready for that European vacation you've always wanted" is much more engaging than "It gives me great pleasure to inform you of the board's decision to approve your request for. . . ."

Tell the good news and say it like you mean it.

The Closing Sentence

What about the closing sentence to each paragraph? Knowing when to end is more important than many writers—but few readers—realize. Writing that ends too soon leaves the reader dissatisfied; writing that seems to never end eventually becomes a bore and, as a result, a failure. Try, then, to put almost as much energy into your closing lines as you did into your opening ones.

The most important thing to remember when closing

any paragraph or series of paragraphs is not to repeat your main points—we heard them before—unless you feel it is absolutely necessary. If you feel you should repeat for purposes of clarity or emphasis, try to give the reader something new as well. Set the reader up for the opening line in the next paragraph or reveal some new insight about what your paragraph has been aiming at all along.

The best endings usually take the reader a bit by surprise. They don't signal with cranking sounds like "In conclusion, the reader can easily see . . ." or "What, then, can we glean from . . . ." The best endings maintain the reader's interest to the last word; they don't allow any of the tension that's been built up to sag. In fact, they usually send the reader off inspired to act.

Look at this ending from Ralph Waldo Emerson's essay on language:

> That which was unconscious truth, becomes, when interpreted and defined in an object, a part of the domain of knowledge—a new weapon in the magazine of power.

Or this conclusion from his discussion of idealism:

> No man is its enemy. It accepts whatsoever befalls, as part of its lesson. It is a watcher more than a doer, and it is a doer, only that it may the better watch.

William Butler Yeats tells us that a finished poem makes a noise like the click of a lid on a perfectly made box. Good closing sentences and good closing paragraphs do the same.

The kinds of paragraphs we write, like so many other things in our lives, are frequently determined by fashion. As I've said, right now short paragraphs are "in" and, generally speaking, are more effective than long paragraphs. Especially when relating vital or complicated information. Nevertheless, the writer who can create clean, clear paragraphs containing only the most essential information will always be in style. These paragraphs may not win any prizes, but they have the kind of beauty we appreciate when we see a short-order cook flip pancakes or a second baseman's toss to first for the easy out. These kinds of paragraphs, like these kinds of action, are immediately understood and appreciated. They call attention not to the writer but to the information that best serves the reader's interests.

SENTENCES

Writing good sentences means no dependent clauses, no dangling things, no flashbacks, and keeping the subject near the predicate. We throw in as many fresh words as we can get away with. Simple, short sentences don't always work. You have to do tricks with pacing, alternate long sentences with short, to keep it vital and alive.

—*Theodore Geisel (Dr. Seuss)*

Clarity, Coherence, and Variety

There are several definitions for a sentence—a complete thought, a unit of expression, a group of words that ends with a period, exclamation point, or question mark—but no definition tells us much about how to write one.

The most effective way to write lively, engaging, powerful sentences is to freewrite (see pages 27–39). Freewriting, once we open up the right sides of our brains, enables our sentences to write themselves. All we have to do is record what our minds dictate. Then, once our thoughts are on paper, we can add form to function without losing the natural energy of our speaking voices.

When changing our freewritten sentences into the kind of prose that, according to Ernest Hemingway, separates architecture from interior decorating, however, the first things we want to look at are (1) clarity, (2) coherence, and (3) variety.

Clarity. Clarity is as necessary to good writing as foundations to houses. It is the basic principle upon which whatever we write—memo or novel—depends. If our ideas aren't understandable, they will be of no use to anyone.

One way of talking about something as abstract as clarity is to look at an example of its opposite:

> Our company is increasingly turning to capacity planning techniques to determine its future processing capability.

This writer wants us to know that the company is preparing to handle more work in the future, but by using words that aren't familiar to every reader, he led one woman to believe he was talking about maternity leaves. By visualizing our readers and using only words that are familiar to them, we can go a long way toward writing sentences that are clearer, simpler, and easier to understand.

Coherence. Coherence is the clear and logical movement from one word to the next. Here are some examples of incoherent sentences:

> Tip O'Neill, the Speaker, and Bob Dole have yet to arrive.

> In the United States, the Soviet Union, China, and now Poland are the most talked about communist countries.

> If you think our employees are rude, you should see the manager.

The easiest way to catch errors in coherence is to proofread out loud. The most effective way to correct them is to divide complicated thoughts into two or more separate sentences.

Variety. Clarity and coherence notwithstanding, too many short sentences put readers to sleep. Where will all our clarity and coherence be then? Whereas one short sentence may be emphatic, three in a row can come across as strained or strident. An occasional one-word sentence can shock or excite, but more than two in a row frequently irritate. See, then, if you can't follow a short sentence with a long one. Ask a question; then exclaim something. Vary the traditional subject, verb, object way of structuring sentences.

You may even wish to break a few rules. Just make sure you do it deliberately and your reader knows you're doing it deliberately. For effect. Writing an incomplete sentence like "For effect" helps vary not only the structure but also the rhythm in your writing. It isolates something to make a stronger point. For another example, look at the way Elie Wiesel uses the incomplete sentence "As usual" in this paragraph from *A Beggar In Jerusalem*:

> We were going to be consumed by fire once more, and once more the world would let it happen. As usual. What was true yesterday will be true tomorrow.

The question to ask when breaking rules is: Does it work? If it works, it's right. If it's interesting, it's correct. Remember, a monotonous style is just as boring as a dull thought.

Two More Considerations

In *Prose Style*, Wilfred Stone tells us of two more things to keep in mind when revising our sentences.

Verbs Are More Important Than Nouns. Because nouns contain information about persons, places, and things, we think of them as the most important words in any message, but nouns lack the power of verbs, so we've fallen into the habit of turning many of our verbs into nouns. We no

longer "count down," for example—we begin a "count-
down." Instead of telling our colleagues, "This book will
help you manage your department better," we tend to write,
"The purpose of this book is improved management techniques." Nouns are important, but substituting them for
verbs only makes our writing heavy and lifeless.

We also try to energize our nouns by turning them into
verbs. Events no longer "have an impact" on our lives; they
"impact" upon them. People are no longer given "tasks";
they're "tasked" to do something. Turning nouns into verbs
can give our writing more power, but the unfamiliar usage
can also distract our readers from the points we wish to
make. It can, at times, even damage our credibility as clear
thinkers and writers.

Personal Is More Engaging Than Impersonal. How many
times have we not cared very much about an earthquake
or some other disaster until we heard of a mother and child
trapped in a building for several days? How many times is
a baseball game made more interesting when we know one
of the players is trying to overcome some physical or mental
handicap? How many times have we read of people gen-
erously responding to the needs of others because of something they read in the newspapers or saw on television?

Most of the sentences we write have people or some
connection with people in them. Some of our sentences
have no room for people: "The Dow Jones rose three points
today." But sentences that can go either way are usually
improved when we put humans in them. "Basketball requires more stamina than baseball," for example, engages
the reader much more effectively when written, "If you
think you have to be in shape to play baseball, wait until
you try basketball."

Putting people in our writing, according to Stone, is no
different from putting them in a television commercial.
Advertisers could show us a bottle of beer and have a voice

explain why we should drink it, but marketing studies have shown that most impulsive buying initiates with consumers who imagine they are like the people they see in advertisements or wish they could be like the people they see in advertisements.

The same holds true in writing. People like to read about and respond to other people. New ideas, for example, are often best presented by introducing readers to the people who created the ideas, showing people who are affected by the ideas, and explaining how these ideas can help those who become acquainted with them.

But it is not enough for us as writers to get out of the way and allow readers to meet and hear people. We have to come across as people too. To do this, we have to develop our own individual writing voices. We have to make our readers feel as if they are listening to a human being.

Reading Level

We hear a lot of talk about writing at the level our readers can understand. Implied in this idea is the notion that all writers are naturally superior to their readers, that all writers have to find ways to lower their standards so their readers can understand them.

Nothing could be further from the truth. More people read more today than ever before, and they are highly skilled. Newspapers, magazines, books, advertising, television, movies: Rarely does a sentence appear that hasn't been crafted by a professional writer. The subjects may be shallow, but the writing is almost always clear, direct, and personal. And clear, direct, personal writing is what our readers have come to expect.

Because we're all insecure about our writing, we tend to hide our insecurity behind big words and convoluted sentence structures. That way, if our readers don't understand what we've written, we can pin the blame on them. We can say they're the ones who are stupid. As readers, we often feel stupid if we can't readily grasp what a writer is trying to say, even if the writing is simply muddled. Instead of recognizing the insecurity of others, our own insecurity makes us feel that we're the ones who failed. It never dawns on us that muddled writing is a sign of a muddled mind and clear writing is a sign of a clear mind.

Here's a test to see how muddled or clear your writing is. Find something you've written that has 150 words in it. Then count the number of words having one syllable. Divide that number by 10. Then subtract your answer from 20. The number you get is the number of years in school your readers need to understand what you've written without its becoming a burden to them.

Most people consider *The New Yorker* and *The Atlantic Monthly* pretty highbrow magazines. What do you think is the grade level at which almost all of their stories are written?

Lower than twelve.

Always.

And no one ever accused James Thurber, Janet Flanner, John Updike, Anne Beattie, E. B. White, John Cheever, Pauline Kael, Woody Allen & Co. of ever talking down to their readers.

Big words aren't the only things that slow our sentences down, however. Convoluted sentence structures, created for the same reason we rush to the thesaurus for big words, also handicap our ability to communicate effectively. And of all the ways we can come up with to make our sentences sound stiff and stuffy, none is used more often than the long, formal introductory clause.

There is nothing wrong with long introductory clauses. I used one in the preceding sentence, which seems to condemn them. But, as in so many of the cases discussed in this book, we tend to rely too heavily on them. They may help us put more information in a sentence or clarify something, but they also have a way of delaying the point we're trying to make. We find ourselves talking *about* a subject before we've said what the subject is.

For example: "Well before *The Public Burning* established his prominence in contemporary fiction, Robert Coover had achieved a reputation for originality and versatility." Notice what happens when we take the main idea in this sentence and put it at the beginning: "Robert Coover had a reputation for originality and versatility long before he established his prominence in contemporary fiction." Without changing many of the words, we have made the sentence more simple, clear, and direct.

PHRASES

> There is but one art . . . to omit. O' if I knew how to omit I would ask no other knowledge. A man who knew how to omit would make an *Iliad* of a daily paper.
>
> —*Robert Louis Stevenson*

Phrases are small groups of words that work together to give more meaning to a sentence:

The man *in the living room* runs a computer business.

He tends *to enjoy his work.*

Getting him to leave his office for a round of golf isn't easy.

Rarely do we write a sentence that doesn't contain some kind of phrase. Perhaps this is the reason why we take such unfair advantage of them. That and the fact that there isn't much to work with in a noun or a verb. Whatever the reasons, phrases are a main target for many frontal assaults on the English language. Instead of writing "then," we say "at that point in time." We prefer "until such time as" to "when," and anything "to be done now" is "to be effective immediately."

These kinds of phrases work against us in two ways. Because they're been used so many times, they're boring. They're not much different from the dreaded cousin who tells the same stories over and over again regardless of the occasion. Phrases of this kind are also dehumanizing. They don't reflect a real person and often make our readers feel diminished, as if they don't deserve an authentic, human voice.

Nevertheless, most of us continue to write this way for two reasons:

It's Safe. Because others write this way, we think it's okay for us to do it too. And if we didn't write like this, our readers would think we were "unprofessional."

There is certainly a great deal of truth to these statements. Many of us work for people who feel nervous about sending anything out of the office that isn't unintelligible. These people have to be slowly, carefully, and patiently educated over a long period of time. They have yet to learn that people who rise to the top don't get there by doing what they're "supposed" to do. The *Harvard Business Review* once conducted a study of 800 letters written by the most prominent chief executive officers in the country. The study revealed many things about the executives, their businesses, and their clients, but the amazing thing about the letters was that all 800 of them had three things in common: They were short, clear, and personal—almost the exact opposite of what we've come to call "professional."

It's Easy. When we begin our letters with "Pursuant to our telephone conversation . . . ," we don't have to think of something to say. And "Enclosed please find . . . ," "Please be advised . . . ," and "In accordance with your request

. . . ," can be called upon to open other paragraphs in our letters. In fact, most of these prefabricated phrases are found at the beginning of our paragraphs and at the end of our closing. We use them to get us going and tell our readers when we're going to stop, but a readymade phrase works against us, because it undermines whatever energy we've created.

We can combat the numbing that prefabricated phrases cause in our readers by using them to get started in our rough drafts and then eliminating them before we begin our final drafts. Most of the time they can be taken out while changing little else in the sentences in which they appear. If, however, the resulting sentences look a little naked or perhaps too blunt, we can often substitute a pronoun for the phrase we don't need. For example, instead of saying, "In accordance with your request . . ." or "Pursuant to our agreement . . . ," we can say, "Your request for . . ." and "We agreed . . . ."

Because prefabricated phrases were created to plug into a wide range of contexts, they tend to be rather general or even vague. See if you can't make them more specific. "Your assistance in this matter has been greatly appreciated," for example, could be changed to "Thank you for finishing those invoices so quickly."

Substituting the particular for the general is also an effective way to reinforce the ways we want our readers to act. "I look forward to seeing those new time cards distributed" will get our readers moving faster and more efficiently than "Please implement the new policy."

Focusing on the specific and replacing vague phrases with pronouns can also be used to eliminate buzz words or jargon. Jargon is created as a language shortcut. Instead of having to waste time using a lot of words to say what they mean, people in similar professions invent code words to communicate their messages clearly and quickly. The idea works as long as the reader and the writer know the same code words. These codes also make those who use them feel special, as if they belong to a privileged society. That social web begins to unravel, however, when important readers aren't familiar with the jargon. Then, what began as a way to communicate more effectively becomes a burden and a bore.

Because we lack confidence in our ability to write well and because most of us tend to follow the path of least resistance when it comes to something we don't like to do, we welcome a cliché whenever we have trouble saying what we mean. Like prefabricated phrases, they're safe and easy. If our readers don't understand them, that's their problem.

If only the problem ended there! We may use clichés, jargon, and buzz words to mask our insecurity, but there are people in this world who use these same kinds of words to play on our insecurity. They know that if we're too lazy to say what we mean, we're probably too lazy to figure out what they mean. And if they repeat their words often enough, we'll even start using them. Then we'll not only be saying what we don't mean, we'll be saying what they mean.

The best examples of this kind of communication come out of Nazi Germany. No government has ever been able to outdo the Third Reich's ingenious methods of camouflaging through language its genocide of the Jewish people. Prisoners sent to concentration camps had to carry identity papers marked "return unwanted." These prisoners were accorded "special treatment." "Return unwanted" and "special treatment" both meant death. So did Adolf Hitler's phrase for these murders: "the final solution."

Though no government has equaled the Nazis' ability to apply harmless labels to hideous practices, some have come close. When the world found out that 30,000 people in Argentina had disappeared or been killed in the 1970s, the ruling military government admitted that in its enthusiasm to repress leftists, "errors were committed that could sometimes trespass the boundaries of respect for fundamental human rights." Ferdinand Marcos' Philippine government had a word for this process of eliminating troublesome people. It was called "salvaging." Those in prison waiting to be salvaged were said to be "tactically immobilized."

But these are obvious examples. What about the not so obvious? They permeate almost every field of interest. Food processors, for example, have taken the term "powdered bone" from packages of bologna, hot dogs, sausages, and hamburger patties and replaced it with the word "calcium." Calcium, which we think of as good for our health, refers in this case to pulverized bone, bone marrow, and connective tissue. Donald Huston of the Department of Agriculture explains: "This action facilitates the use of mechanically separated meat while continuing to assure customers they have wholesome, unadulterated meat products that are properly labeled."

Several years ago, the Justice Department filed a suit against the accounting firm Ernst and Whinney for intentionally using "false, misleading, and deceptive" language on a client's Internal Revenue form. The purpose of this language was to qualify the client for tax credits. Here are some of the verbal tricks Ernst and Whinney's accountants came up with: they listed a fire alarm bell as a "combustion enunciator," doors as "movable partitions," and windows as "decorative features." An entire refrigerated warehouse, on the other hand, became a "freezer," and ninety-two cubic yards of topsoil came out as a "planter." In their defense, Ernst and Whinney claimed they were only trying "to put their client's best foot forward."

Irresponsible Language

Aside from their own considerable resourcefulness, writers whose purpose is to deceive, evade, confuse, and mislead rely on a number of proven techniques:

Euphemism. We use euphemisms when we want to hide something. When someone dies, we try to avoid the pain by saying that the person has "passed away." Sometimes our attempts to avoid reality are comical, as when morticians refer to their work as "the last step in the health-care delivery system," but most political and social abuses of the language are pernicious. In fact, the degree of inhumanity in many destructive acts is usually directly proportionate to the language created to cover them up. In his essay "Politics and the English Language," George Orwell tells us:

> Millions of peasants are robbed of their farms and sent trudging along the roads with no more than they can carry: this is called "transfer of population" or "rectification of frontiers." People are imprisoned for years without trial, or shot in the back of the neck or sent to die of scurvy in Arctic lumber camps: this is called "elimination of undesirable elements." Such phraseology is needed if we want to name things without calling up mental images of them.

Orwell then goes on to show us how a college professor might defend these atrocities. He wouldn't just say, "I believe it's okay to kill people if good things can come from it." He'd sound much more like this: "While freely conceding that the Soviet regime exhibits certain features that the humanitarian may be inclined to deplore, we must, I think, agree that a certain curtailment of the right to political opposition is an unavoidable concomitant of transitional periods."

Follow Orwell's advice: Be suspicious of words that don't bring a picture to mind. "Pacification," "protecting the peace," and "terminate with extreme prejudice" do not create an image of bound, blindfolded, kneeling prisoners with pistols held to their heads. Nor do we hear the shots, see the bodies lurch forward, or feel the blood splattering in every direction.

Doubletalk. Another form of concealment, doubletalk avoids an issue by talking around it. When teachers at Milwaukee Area Technical College asked why they were offered only a 3 percent salary increase when the college's director received a 13 percent pay raise after only one year on the job, a trustee told them, "What's being offered you is an economic package. What's being offered Dr. Slicher is a specific comment on his performance."

Asked whether it was proper for the Central Intelligence Agency to support a covert war and whether the American people had a right to know of the agency's role, President Ronald Reagan replied, "Covert actions have been a part of government and a part of government's responsibilities for as long as there's been a government. I do believe in the right of a country when it believes that its interests are best served to practice covert activity and then—while you people have a right to know, you can't let your people know without letting the wrong people know—those that may oppose what you're doing."

Gobbledygook. The point of gobbledygook is to overwhelm the reader with nonsense. Make him or her feel that any attempt to understand or be understood is hopeless. Welfare recipients in England, for example, are told, "Within the housing benefit granted to you there has been an amount of transitional addition; this was granted to compensate for higher non-dependent charges."

And what do you think readers of publications put out by the United States Office of Education make of this simpler explanation of a complex idea: "In other words, feediness in the shared information between toputness and inputness, where toputness is at a time just prior to inputness."

Even when we want to help, we sometimes wind up causing more confusion than anything else. Imagine the time and effort that must have been devoted to this sentence in an anatomy textbook: "The lateral surface, lateral to the anterior border, is anterior, lateral, and also posterior above, for it extends from the anterior to the posterior border of the radial tuberosity, but is largely lateral below, and the posterior surface, narrow and mostly medial above, expands and is truly posterior below."

Neologisms. In other words, new words. The nuclear power industry sweeps all the awards here. Explosions in nuclear reactors are called "energetic disassemblies," and fires are referred to as "rapid oxidation." In fact, the Batelle Corporation is in the middle of a campaign to change the way people think about nuclear accidents. If all goes according to plan, by the year 2002, we will respond to them the same way we respond to hurricanes, earthquakes, tidal waves, and other natural disasters. Answering charges that Batelle's campaign was one-dimensionally "pro-nuclear," a representative of the company replied that it was a "pro-education program," and that anti-nuclear resistance "damaged the cause of public knowledge and intelligence about energy information for all time."

But back to neologisms. We haven't always "optimized," "randomized," "finalized," and "federalized"; we used to decide, choose, act, and resolve. Not too long ago, people used to meet; now they "interface" to seek "measurable end products" they can "prioritize" and eventually "effectuate" in some "out year."

Bafflegab. Bafflegab is what we resort to when nothing else works. Bafflegab combines elements of all the other techniques but is somehow, if possible, beyond them. If there were a Lewis Carroll Award for "multisyllabic circumlocution," all the contestants would be bafflegabbers.

Some bafflegab, like the Pentagon's calling a pencil a "portable hand-held communications inscriber," is funny; other bafflegab is pathetic—the Reagan administration's refusal to admit that the invasion of Grenada was an invasion, for instance: Spokespersons called it everything from a "rescue mission" to a "pre-dawn vertical insertion."

A more sophisticated example of bafflegab is the term "national species of special emphasis." Endangered species, as we all know, are in danger of extinction and are protected by law from being killed. "National species of special emphasis," however, are endangered species we can kill legally.

Resisting Deceptive Language

Euphemisms, doubletalk, gobbledygook, neologisms, and bafflegab make up a language of nonresponsibility. Those who use it eliminate serious discussion of any issue because their whole intent is to prevent, confuse, and conceal clear thinking without accepting any blame for the chaos that follows. Whenever caught in the mire they have created or questioned about the trouble they may have caused, these dark evaders never admit to having made a mistake. The best we can get of them is that they "misspoke" themselves.

The most effective way to resist this language of deceit is to be skeptical. Of ourselves as well as others. Ernest Hemingway tells us that the most essential gift for a good writer is a built-in, shock-proof shit detector.

How good is yours? If you react automatically and predictably to terms like "abortion," "terrorism," and "AIDS," you may be in danger of manipulating yourself or allowing others to manipulate you. Becoming aware of your deepest convictions, your habitual responses to certain issues, is the first step toward protecting yourself. This doesn't mean that you should change your opinions, only that you should be aware of how strongly you hold them. The tighter the hold, the more vulnerable you are to deceiving yourself and passively or uncritically deceiving others.

Want to test your shit detector? Read the following statements collected by Jean Ward, a journalism professor at the University of Minnesota. Put a "yes" in front of any statement that reflects or confirms a bias. Write "no" before any statements that are free of presumptions. Don't study them; just record your immediate response: "yes" or "no."

_____ The documentary delightfully explores the rivalries between different orchestral sections, as well as some of the personal ones, like the feud between a woman cellist who takes nips from a whiskey bottle and a violinist she accuses of molesting little girls.
—*Minneapolis Tribune*, 14 November 1979

_____ An Illinois man and wife were charged here Tuesday with illegal possession and intent to sell about 12 pounds of hashish worth about $30,000.
—Associated Press, 11 October 1979

_____ To her neighbors in the Baltimore suburb of Towson, Maryland, Jean M. Krik is simply a pleasant, church-going, working housewife and mother of four. But then there's the R. Rowe Price Associates Inc. business card that carries the title of assistant vice president.
—*Wall Street Journal*, 13 November 1979

_____ The death penalty will be sought against a 24-year-old South Side man who pleaded guilty Tuesday to kidnapping, raping, and murdering a doctor's wife last year, prosecutors said.
—*Chicago Tribune*, 10 October 1979

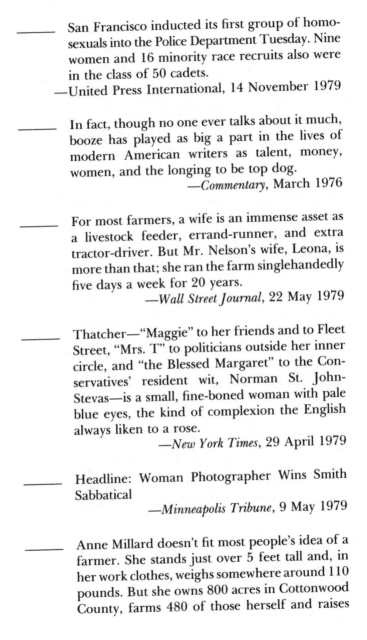

_____ San Francisco inducted its first group of homo-sexuals into the Police Department Tuesday. Nine women and 16 minority race recruits also were in the class of 50 cadets.

—United Press International, 14 November 1979

_____ In fact, though no one ever talks about it much, booze has played as big a part in the lives of modern American writers as talent, money, women, and the longing to be top dog.

—*Commentary*, March 1976

_____ For most farmers, a wife is an immense asset as a livestock feeder, errand-runner, and extra tractor-driver. But Mr. Nelson's wife, Leona, is more than that; she ran the farm singlehandedly five days a week for 20 years.

—*Wall Street Journal*, 22 May 1979

_____ Thatcher—"Maggie" to her friends and to Fleet Street, "Mrs. T" to politicians outside her inner circle, and "the Blessed Margaret" to the Conservatives' resident wit, Norman St. John-Stevas—is a small, fine-boned woman with pale blue eyes, the kind of complexion the English always liken to a rose.

—*New York Times*, 29 April 1979

_____ Headline: Woman Photographer Wins Smith Sabbatical

—*Minneapolis Tribune*, 9 May 1979

_____ Anne Millard doesn't fit most people's idea of a farmer. She stands just over 5 feet tall and, in her work clothes, weighs somewhere around 110 pounds. But she owns 800 acres in Cottonwood County, farms 480 of those herself and raises

chickens, hogs, and cattle. Not bad for a 60-year-old widow.
—*Minneapolis Tribune*, 5 December 1976

—— The Etelsons were married in 1950, and for the first years of their marriage, Mrs. Etelson operated a cafeteria in an industrial plant. She stopped working between 1958 and 1961 to care for her two young daughters.
—*Wall Street Journal*, 4 May 1978

—— Mundal, Norway—On a summer's day in 1856, a farmer named Frederick Mundal, his wife, and their 6-year-old son, Ole, set out on a long and perilous journey.
—*New York Times*, 16 April 1979

If you wrote "yes" before each statement, you did well. If you realized that every statement reflects and reinforces some stereotype about women, your detector is ticking at just the right speed. If you noticed that almost all of these statements appeared in a single year, move on to the next chapter. The rest of us will try to match the statements with the stereotypes listed below:

1. All people are male unless proven female.

2. A woman is defined by her relationship to a man.

3. A woman's appearance requires comment, whether she defies or exemplifies a popular stereotype.

4. A woman can be safely identified as "his wife"; it is unnecessary to identify her by name.

5. After marriage, a man remains a man and a woman becomes a wife.

6. Homemaking and parenting aren't work.

7. It is newsworthy when a church member, parent, and neighbor is successful in business or the professions, provided the successful person is a woman.

8. Status as housewife takes precedence over all other kinds of status.

9. Events in a woman's life must be identified as A.M. (Ante-Marriage) and P.M. (Post-Marriage).

No answers provided for this test. If you aren't sure which stereotypes apply to which statements (some reflect more than one), you have another measurement of how easy it is for you to deceive yourself on this issue or allow yourself to be deceived by others.

Although we are all very good at recognizing biases in others, we're not always adept at realizing prejudices in ourselves or the people who think like us. We can't help that many of us were brought up to see men and women in rigid, often negative ways, but we can do something about it.

The first step is to become aware of how we really feel about issues. Take this problem of sexist discrimination in language. Do you refer to men as "men" but women as "girls"? Do you have a tendency to say "lady doctor" or "lady lawyer"? Do you begin letters with "Gentlemen" or "Dear Sir"? Do you call women by their first names and men by their last, even though they hold similar positions where you work? Do you perpetuate the idea that women aren't fit for certain kinds of work by using words like "spokesman" or "repairman"? Do you think it's bad form to make others feel uncomfortable by not laughing at a "dirty" joke? Do you think all the fuss about sexist writing is trivial?

If you answered "yes" to more than a few of these questions, you're going to need more than a new vocabulary. You need help in becoming more sensitive to the effects of discrimination in language. While having your consciousness raised, however, you can avoid offending others by incorporating the following suggestions into your writing.

Avoid Sexist Language

Try to convince yourself that "man" is no longer a generic term. If it ever really was, according to Ellen Raddish, we wouldn't have problems with a statement like "Modern man no longer pampers himself during pregnancy. He leads an active life and often continues at his job right up to the day he goes into labor and gives birth."

Here are some suggestions the Canadian government has come up with for at least making people believe we no longer hold our old prejudices:

USE PARALLEL LANGUAGE

Instead of:	*Write:*
men and ladies	men and women; gentlemen and ladies
man and wife	man and woman; husband and wife
Roger Giroux and Jane	Roger Giroux and Jane Ward

USE TERMS THAT INCLUDE BOTH SEXES

Instead of:	*Write:*
mankind	people
all men	all people
chairman	chairperson; chair; head
manned	staffed
average man	average person

Instead of:	Write:
policeman	police officer
fireman	firefighter
newsman	reporter; journalist
male nurse	nurse
lady doctor	doctor

USE PLURAL FORMS

Instead of: Each chairman must meet with his staff.

Write: Chairpersons must meet with their staffs.

USE "THE," "A," OR "AN"

Instead of: Each chairman must submit his report of the meeting.

Write: Each chair must submit a report of the meeting.

USE "YOU"

Instead of: Every chairman wants to prove himself.

Write: As head of the department, you want to prove yourself.

What about "Mr.," "Mrs." "Ms.," and "Miss"? How do you know when to use which? The Canadian government suggests:

• Find out how people like to be addressed. Some people prefer to be called by their first name.

• If using first names proves awkward, use "Mr." for men and "Ms." for women. If a woman wants to be called "Mrs." or "Miss," she can let you know when she signs her name to a letter. If the person you're writing to has a title like "Dr." or "Professor," you can sidestep the "Ms.," "Mrs.," or "Miss" issues.

- Don't use "Gentlemen" or "Dear Sir" unless you're absolutely sure that everyone who reads what you've written is male. There are legions of women and more than a few men who throw these letters away without reading a word.

- If you can't determine your reader's gender, write "Dear Sir or Madam" or "Dear Mr. or Ms." If all you have to go by are initials and a last name, write "Dear J. A. Myers."

One General Rule. Ignore gender unless necessary or appropriate. In "The woman driver told the court," the use of "woman" reflects and confirms a prejudice against drivers who happen to be women. "The first woman appointed," on the other hand, calls attention to an important moment in the history of a company, institution, or country.

As in the case of gender, mention race, age, and disability only when necessary. Instead of writing "disadvantaged black children," for example, "disadvantaged children" or "children from lower-income families" might prevent readers from believing that the children are disadvantaged because they're black. Similarly, a person's ethnic background should be mentioned only if it is relevant. How important, for instance, is it for us to know that Ronald Reagan is Irish or Mario Cuomo Italian?

Journalists almost always include a person's age in their stories, but rarely is it necessary. In business, it almost always isn't. Sandra Day O'Connor's appointment to the Supreme Court has little to do with her age, but the fact that she's the first woman to sit on the Court is important to note.

Writers often reveal their own biases and contribute to misunderstanding in others by using the words "disability" and "handicapped" interchangeably. A "disability" is some kind of physical or emotional impairment; a "handicap" occurs when disabled people can't overcome certain obstacles or barriers. A person in a wheelchair, for example, is "handicapped" in certain physical situations; a person who has learned to deal with a "learning disability" is no longer "handicapped."

When we feel that a person's disabilities or handicaps should be mentioned, however, some ways of mentioning them are more considerate than others. For example, a sentence beginning "An epileptic, Michael Grabowski still manages to perform well. . . ." calls more attention to Michael's epilepsy than it does to his performance. A more sensitive and accurately focused sentence might begin, "Michael Grabowski has never allowed epilepsy to stand in his way."

Enough said. On to "Words."

WORDS

Seize the subject and the words will follow.
—Cato the Elder

The first and most important thing to remember about words is that the most effective are the ones that are yours, the words you speak every day. You've tested these words. You know what they say about you and how people respond when you use them. The biggest mistake you can make as a writer is to write the way you think writing should sound. Write the way *you* sound.

Reading, regardless of the number of people who read a particular letter or story, is still a personal, private act between two people: the reader and the writer. And as in most other relationships, our readers like to know whom they are spending time with. So let your personality shine through your writing. Allow your readers to feel as if a human being and not some machine is speaking to them. The more you are you in your writing, the more likely your readers will be to listen to and agree with what you have to say. If you have a sense of humor, let that humor come through. If you have some favorite expressions you use when speaking, use them when you write as well. They'll help your readers understand what you want to say because you know how to say what you mean. Writing is no different from life. The real you is the one people respond to best.

Freewriting (see pages 27–39) is the most effective technique for getting your words on paper. What they reveal about you—either intentionally or accidentally—is, in large part, what constitutes your style, what separates you from all other writers.

Rewriting (see pages 40–64) helps you fine-tune your already lively and engaging style. It helps you get your message across more effectively without taking anything away from who you are. Just as you use words to say what you have to say, your readers need words to help them understand better what you've said. The more you can help them, the easier it will be to convince them to do what you want.

Guidelines for Increasing the Impact of Words

Here are some guidelines for making the words we use naturally have a stronger impact on our readers.

Use Short Words. Short words are easier to read, and we understand them quickly. Only the insecure—and superiority is only one way of revealing insecurity—try to impress people with a big vocabulary. The best writers know that their job is to choose words to help their readers, not send them running to the dictionary.

Rudolf Flesch, who gave us the *Poor Writer's Almanac* that begins this chapter, once planned to write a thesaurus for people who wanted to simplify their styles. He formed a panel of twelve leaders from twelve different fields and gave them a list of long, pompous words. Then he asked them to figure out how often they used these words. The only time any of the leaders used any of the words on Flesch's list was when they parodied people who used big words. If they said "alleviate your concern" for "don't worry," for example, they made sure their readers knew they were joking.

Flesch never wrote his thesaurus, but with the help of his panel, he did come up with a list of the most commonly used big words. These words were also the most abused. Rarely did they say what the people who used them meant. Take the case of "anticipate" used for "expect." When we "expect" something, we think it's going to happen. "Anticipate" means something stronger. "Anticipate" means we act in a way that is based on something we know will happen. A person who "expects" rain is not surprised when he feels a few drops on his head; someone who "anticipates" rain leaves home with an umbrella. "Substantial," on the other hand, can mean "big," but it can also mean "considerable," "ample," "important," and "of moment." In other words, "substantial" has connotations that can change or dilute the meaning of "big." If we mean "big," we should say "big."

Now Flesch isn't saying we shouldn't use any of the big words on his list. On some occasions, they will be the best words. What Flesch is saying is that we should avoid substituting big words for little words; we should rely on the words we use when we speak.

Here are some of the words on Flesch's list. The words in the parentheses are ones we are most likely to speak and that we seem to forget whenever we write:

advise (write)   in the event that (if)
ascertain (find out)   locate (find)
assist (help)   obtain (get)
comply (follow)   personnel (people)
cooperate (help)   presently (now)
disclose (show)   prior to (before)
endeavor (try)   pursuant to (under)
facilitate (make easy)   represent (be)
failed to (didn't)   require (need)
forward (send)   state (say)
inasmuch as (since)   submit (give, send)
indicate (say, show)   subsequent (later)

Use Clear Words. Use words that are easy to pronounce and everyone can understand. Long and unfamiliar words slow readers down, and readers who slow down often stop. "Illumination on these premises must be extinguished after nightfall" hangs on a wall in Macy's department store in New York City. Some of the employees think it means they shouldn't smoke.

Beware of jargon and slang. These words are clear only to a few. Let them live in your minds and they will think your thoughts for you, construct your sentences for you, and eventually hide what you mean from you as well as from your readers.

Also keep an eye out for words that sound alike but have different meanings. "There," "their," and "they're" and "to," "two," and "too" are the most commonly confused of these kinds of words. Because we know what they mean and how to spell them, we take them for granted. Our eyes pass over them when we proofread, and so do machines with spelling checks. If you have trouble with these words, ask a friend or colleague to proofread what you've written.

Here are some other words we tend to substitute for one another.

Affect, Effect. In common speech (that is, not in psychology writing), *affect* is a verb. It means "to bring about a change, to stimulate, to influence." *Effect* can be a verb or a noun. As a verb, it means "to cause"; as a noun, it means "a result."

Don't let his moods *affect* you.

Will they *effect* a resolution?

The *effect* of his work can be seen in the mailroom.

Assure, Ensure, Insure. To *assure* is "to speak confidently about something." To *ensure* is "to make certain, to guarantee." To *insure* is "to protect with insurance against loss or damage."

I *assure* you, your check is in the mail.

To *ensure* a good seat, buy your ticket now.

You need to *insure* your house.

Couldn't Care Less, Could Care Less. *Couldn't care less* means you care so little about something, it would be impossible for you to care less. *Could care less* is an expression that came from people hearing—or, rather, not hearing—the *n't* in *couldn't care less*. *Could care less* means that you do care a little bit. *Couldn't care less* is a complete absence of concern.

I *couldn't care less* about his promotion.

Different From, Different Than. *Different from* tells us the difference between two or more people, places, or things. *Different than* is used when the object is a clause, to avoid wordiness.

His views are *different from* mine.

My views are *different than* they used to be.

Farther, Further. *Farther* has to do with distance; *further* is matter of degree. *Further* can also be used as a verb meaning "to promote" or "to advocate."

She lives *farther* from me than you.
The *further* into debt he goes, the more irritable he gets.
To *further* the cause of equal rights is a noble ambition.

Fewer, Less. *Fewer* has to do with numbers; *less* has to do with quantity.

Fewer people attended this year's meeting. (To use *less* in this case would mean that the people were missing something, like arms or legs.)
People are eating *less* and *less* sugar these days and smoking *fewer* and *fewer* cigarettes.

Hopefully. Few words upset the office grammarian or frustrated English teacher as much as *hopefully* when it is used to express our or someone else's hoping.

Hopefully, we won't be kept too long.

People who know everything there is to know about our language except how to enjoy it want us to say, "I hope" or "Let's hope" or anything other than *hopefully*. On the other hand, these same people see nothing wrong with saying, "*Admittedly, hopefully* is an obsession of mine."

Lie, Lay. To *lie* is to rest or recline, as in

We *lie* down.

To *lay* is to put or place something down, as in

Lay your report on my desk.

But the ways we use these words aren't as simple as their definitions. In "We *lay* on the grass," for example, *lay* is the past tense of *lie*. H. W. Fowler tells us that *lay* and *lain* can stem from *lie*, but *laid* never can. *Laid*, according to Fowler, can come only from *lay*. Apparently, Fowler never *laid* on the grass or anywhere else. And, of course, this *lie* and *lay* must never be confused with the other *lie* and *lay*, the false statement and the song. *Lay*, of course, may also be used in a sexual context as either a verb or a noun. How do we tell them all apart? Read out loud the sentences in which they appear. Rarely will we go wrong. Also, the verb *lay*, meaning "to put," always takes an object. Something has to be placed somewhere. The verb *lie*, on the other hand, never requires an object.

Reason Is Because, Reason Is That. *Reason is because* is considered redundant because both *reason* and *because* have to do with cause. *Reason is that* is the grammatically correct expression.

The reason is that I prefer not to.

Try To, Try And. To *try to* means "to make an attempt." To *try and* implies that two separate actions are taking place: the *try* and whatever verb comes after it.

Try to read more; it will help your writing.

The best book for distinguishing these kinds of words from one another is H. W. Fowler's *Dictionary of Modern English Usage*. It also makes for some fascinating reading in its own right. Did you know, for example, that Yiddish is not a kind of Hebrew but a kind of German? That *y* used to be interchangeable with *i*? That *w* was once *uu*? That a fuse is called a "fuse" not because it fuses but because it's spindle-shaped? That "belfry" is not named from "bell"?

That "Welsh rabbit" is amusing and right and "Welsh rare-bit" is stupid and wrong? That "isle" and "island" have nothing in common? That "protagonist" is not the opposite of "antagonist"? Find the answer to these and other mysteries of our language in Fowler, the best book on usage ever printed.

Use Concrete Words. Use words that mean something, words for which there are no synonyms. When we speak, we have hands, eyes, and tones of voice to make up for words that don't carry much weight. Take the word "love," for example. We can say we loved the party, fell in love, and would love to go horseback riding because our hands, eyes, and intonations help our listeners understand exactly what we mean. But without these gestures and intonations, words like "love" lose their power. They're like shooting blanks; they make a sound but they have no effect on the target. When we write about love, we have to find words and images that embody feeling: Deborah, Boston, Beacon Hill, 1980, the Fourth of July, the rusted Volkswagen, the kiss by the canal.

Writers have to search for words their readers can feel. Words like "politician," "to," and "now," for example, say more than "representative," "proceed," and "at this point in time." To say someone is "immature" is not nearly so effective as to say the person is "forty going on thirteen." "Slums" creates a more vivid image in our readers' minds than "inner-city housing," "beating children" tells our readers what "corporal punishment" really is, and the "saturation bombing of civilians" should be more difficult to ignore than "air support."

Which words are the best to use depends on the subject and the audience. The important thing to remember is that most people don't usually think in abstract terms but in concrete particulars. Given words that are general or vague, readers tend to create their own images of what the writer means. Good writers, then, don't let their readers fill in their prose for them. They find the words for the images they want their readers to have. In his *Philosophy of Style*, Herbert Spencer says that if we find ourselves writing sentences like "In proportion as the manners, customs, and amusements of a nation are cruel and barbarous, the regulations of their penal code will be severe," we should consider alternatives such as "In proportion as men delight in battles, bullfights, and combats of gladiators, will they punish by hanging, burning, and the rack."

Avoid Unnecessary Words. When we freewrite, we think about *what* we want to say; when we rewrite, we think about *how* we want to say it. We search for the most effective words to express what we mean, but even these words, as powerful as they may be, weaken when surrounded by unnecessary ones.

Notice the energy that is lost when the words listed below have to carry the weight of those that have little meaning or repeat the meaning of the main word:

analysis	final analysis
basics	basic fundamentals
because	because of the fact that
brief	brief in duration
consensus	consensus of opinion
during 1987	during the year 1987
effect	resulting effect
except	with the exception of
few	few in number
just	just recently
maximum	greatest maximum possible
meet	meet together
merge	merge together
nominated	nominated for the position of
one hour	one hour of your time

problem	unresolved problem
repeat	repeat the same
smile	smile on his face
study	make a study of
surplus	surplus left over
the question	the question as to whether
until	until such time as
warning	advance warning

Some phrases, similar to the redundancies in the right-hand column above, can be eliminated completely from our writing, thus giving more power to the words we keep. "I would like to ask you," for example, can probably be replaced by the asking. And anything "needless to say" probably doesn't need to be said.

Write in the Active Voice. Active words move our readers along; passive words slow them down:

Passive: The street was crossed by the chicken.

Active voice puts the chicken and the street where they belong:

Active: The chicken crossed the street.

Here are some other advantages to writing in the active rather than the passive voice:

ACTIVE VOICE IS MORE EMPHATIC. "I expect to meet the deadline" has a ring of conviction that "The deadline is expected to be met" obviously lacks.

ACTIVE VOICE IS MORE PERSONAL. "It has been brought to my attention that you have been late for work recently" isn't nearly as direct or as forceful as "I hear you were late again."

ACTIVE VOICE IS MORE RESPONSIBLE. Rarely do politicians say, "We made a mistake." If they did, they might lose the next election. What politicians and those who wish to avoid responsibility for their actions say is, "A mistake was made."

Nevertheless, there are times when passive voice is more effective than active:

PASSIVE VOICE FOCUSES THE READER'S ATTENTION AWAY FROM WHOEVER IS DOING THE ACTION. "Your application for the marketing position *has been carefully reviewed* by the search committee" has the reader thinking about what happened to the application rather than anything the writer may have done. If this is going to be a letter of rejection, the writer is not going to receive the full force of the reader's response. In other words, the focus on the application serves to deflect the reader both from him- or herself and from the writer.

PASSIVE VOICE CAN SOFTEN A BLOW. "Unfortunately, it did not meet all of the criteria *established by the president.*" It *is* a letter of rejection, but again the focus of attention is on the application; the reader doesn't feel as if he or she has been personally rejected. Or at least not as much as if the writer had used the word "you" and written in the active voice.

PASSIVE VOICE RELINQUISHES RESPONSIBILITY. "An offer *cannot be made* to you at this time" lets the reader know that the writer is not responsible for the rejection. That has been determined by the president and the members of the Search Committee.

Sometimes the writer doesn't know who is responsible. "The fire alarm was set off by mistake," for example, almost necessitates passive voice. On the other hand, passive voice can be used to shield others. "All the alternatives have been exhausted" sounds better to stockholders than "Your board of directors failed again."

Use Words That Act. There are a lot of fat nouns out there that used to be lean, healthy, active verbs. Give these words life again by freeing them from the "-ion," "-tion," or "-ance" that weighs them down. "The purpose of this magazine is the collection and distribution of news stories," for example, contains a couple of actionless nouns screaming to be recycled. Well, they've come to the right place: "This magazine collects and distributes the news."

Here are some more noun smotherers and the verbs we can free from them:

anticipation	anticipate
conclusion	conclude
consideration	consider
cooperation	cooperate
embarrassment	embarrass
establishment	establish
exaggeration	exaggerate
installation	install
objection	object
promotion	promote
protection	protect
revelation	reveal

Nouns that come from verbs have their place, but too many of them weigh down our prose. The more fat we can trim, the more energy we preserve.

Also, it should be noted, there are more than a few nouns that look awfully uncomfortable as verbs (though "stress" and "task" are okay if sentence "crafting" is okay):

accessorize	stress
deplane	task
finalize	utilize
prioritize	

Nouns made from verbs and verbs made from nouns may sound fancy to the people who use them, but in most cases they come off as an attempt to turn something simple into something complex.

Use Positive Words. Eliminate or change any negative language you can. Unless, of course, you really want to make someone feel bad. Then you can go as far as you think is necessary. Most of the time, however, negative language merely invites a negative response.

Fortunately, positive language is very much in fashion these days. Have you noticed how many stores no longer post signs saying, "We close at nine o'clock"? Now the signs say, "We stay open until nine o'clock." Staying open sounds more positive than closing; it implies that the store is there to serve us. And consider this notice from one Canadian police department:

St. JOHN'S, NEWFOUNDLAND
North America's Oldest City
WELCOMES YOU
You have violated a Parking Regulation;
however, we wish you to
PARK AS LONG AS NECESSARY
We hope you enjoy your stop in St. John's.
Visit our excellent shops, restaurants, theatres,
hotels, churches, and libraries.
PLEASE RETURN AGAIN SOON.
City of St. John's
Traffic Enforcement Division
ANY COURTESY WE CAN EXTEND TO YOU
WILL BE A PLEASURE

As with so much else in this world, however, even this good thing can be overdone, and what we intended to be positive can come off as artificial, contrived, and insincere.

A store near where I live, for example, changed "No out-of-state checks accepted" to "We enthusiastically embrace local checks." A friend visiting from Hungary and not knowing the spelling of many of our words thought the store also served as a center for political refugees.

Here are some words that can turn people off or make them feel defensive:

allege	insist
claim	misinform
complain	mistake
criticize	neglect
error	never
fail	no
fault	overlook
inadequate	oversight
inferior	you must

Here are some words people enjoy reading:

admire	gratitude
agree	pleasure
benefit	satisfy
comfort	thank you
congratulations	value
deserve	welcome
gladly	yes

Consider the effect of the negative words in the following expression. How could they be improved?

Don't smoke in . . .

Don't blame us if . . .

The error is yours . . .

If you would only cooperate . . .

I apologize for the minor problem you had with . . .

No refunds after five days.

You claim in your letter that . . .

Your attitude surprises us.

These expressions, and a few of them contain only positive words, suggest that the reader is careless, stupid, difficult to work with, unappreciative, unreasonable, and a
liar. And in the single case where the writer admits the
reader has a basis for his or her complaint, the value of
that complaint is negated by calling it "minor."

While considering the connotations of positive and negative words, you may want to look out for words that carry
different meanings to different people. A "switch hitter,"
a term derived from baseball, can mean a person who can
do the same job several different ways, but today a "switch
hitter" can also be a person who is sexually active with both
men and women.

Use Personal Words. The fashion when most of us learned
to write was not to call attention to ourselves or others, to
substitute the word "one" anytime we referred to "you" or
"me" or "him" or "her." Fortunately, this formal, distanced,
impersonal word has fallen out of favor. Humanizing words
like "I," "you," "he," "she," "we," "they," "me," "him," "her,"
"your," "our," "their," "mine," "yours," "his," "hers," and
"theirs" are the latest rage. They're also more effective in
drawing the reader into our messages. Compare "Your van
will meet you at 9 o'clock" with "One's van arrives at 9
o'clock." The first sentence makes the reader feel special,
as if the van is his or hers or at least is being sent exclusively
for him or her. The second sentence creates visions of a
long ride to the airport, and it won't matter if the reader
is on the van or not.

Having been rescued from the impersonal "one," however, we have to be careful not to misue "I" and "me." As children, we were corrected every time we said, "Mary and me are going to the store." "Mary and *I*," our parents told us, and sometimes they wouldn't let us out of the house until we repeated the correct version. Unfortunately, we repeated the corrected phrases so many times we now tend to use "I" whenever we join it with someone else's name. "I" is correct *only* when it serves as the subject of some verb. As the object of a verb or preposition, that "I" should be changed to "me." We would never say, for example, "Thanks for inviting I to the party." To say "Thanks for inviting John and I" is equally inappropriate. The correct response is "Thanks for inviting John and me." *you subject simple*

How can you tell when to use "I" and when to use "me"? Take the other person out of the sentence and read the sentence out loud. First with "I" and then with "me." There'll be no doubt about which word is correct.

Another pronoun to be wary of is "myself." Most of the time it is either unnecessary or awkward. "I myself answered that call," for example, is redundant. "The proposal submitted by Mike and myself was approved" takes the perfectly good "me" out of the sentence and puts in its place the inflated, self-conscious "myself." Being put in positions where our egos are at stake, we resort to this kind of writing. Would we ever say, "Thanks for inviting myself to the party"? For the same reason, avoid substituting "myself" for "me." Most of the time, "myself" is awkward and inflated and calls attention to our own lack of confidence.

A final way to make our writing more personal is to use contractions. They've enjoyed a considerable rise in status in the past few years because, like pronouns and a distinct writing voice, they draw the reader quickly and more deeply into whatever we write. And because we use so many contractions when we speak, we're more comfortable with them in print than the previously formal (now stuffy) practice of writing out the individual words that form the contraction.

Be Consistent. Unless you have some good reasons for doing otherwise, maintain the same verb tense throughout each paragraph you write. If you begin a paragraph in the present tense, stay in the present tense until the paragraph is complete. If you want to switch to past or future tense, begin a new paragraph.

The same goes for pronouns. If you start with "you," don't switch to "we" or "I" or anything else unless you're sure of the effect it will have. If you've written a paragraph containing both the formal "one" and the informal "I," make all the pronouns one or the other.

And don't use the word "we" when you mean "I." Even if you're being consistent. Mark Twain tells us there are only three kinds of people who can say "we" and mean "I": kings, editors, and people with tapeworms.

Avoid "Headline" Words. These are words that, for reasons of space, newspaper editors have shortened or changed in some way. Many of these words, abbreviations, and acronyms may be inappropriate outside the newspaper. Say "Republican Party," for example, instead of "GOP." "General Motors," "United States," "United Nations," and "Soviet Union" work more effectively and in some cases more accurately than "GM," "America," "UN," and "Russia." Same goes for "PO" and "KO."

Words that have been shortened are tougher to call because many of them have entered the writing mainstream. Few people, for example, know that "quote" is a shortened form of "quotation." And hardly anybody remembers the original of "taxi:" "taximeter cabriolet." "Recap" for "recapitulation," on the other hand, is still waiting to break out of the newsroom. Also hovering on the threshold of more widespread acceptance are: "alot" and "alright." "Al-

right," in fact, will only have to wait until the next edition
of Webster's *American Heritage Dictionary* to be all right.

As for abbreviations and acronyms, try to use them as
little as possible. A page splattered with capital letters often
unnerves and confuses the reader. If you must use abbreviations or acronyms, make sure you say what they mean
the first time you use each one. This can be done by spelling
the word out the first time it appears and then placing in
parentheses immediately afterwards the initials by which
you'll refer to this word throughout the rest of whatever
you write: " . . .gross national product (GNP)."

Avoid Clichés. Everyone uses clichés or fashionable
expressions, but writers try to keep them at a minimum.
They date what we write and are often inappropriate. Any
Verdi opera, for example, may be "awesome"—but a TV
sit-com? On the other hand, opera will never be "cool,"
although it can be "gross," but that's all determined by what
you think is "tubular." You wouldn't want to "blow out"
anything "tubular."

If clichés slip into your freewriting (which is the only
place they belong), see if you can't replace them with words
that will quickly form images in our readers' minds. Words
like "slap" and "slash" and "slam," for example, create images of distinct action in our minds. The more vivid our
words, the clearer the images; the clearer the images, the
greater the impact; the greater the impact, the swifter and
more thorough the action.

Use a Dictionary. In *Writing Well* the poet Donald Hall
tells us we have to respect words if we're going to express
them honestly. To do this, it helps to develop an affection
for words, to find pleasure in the richness of "hogwash"
or the strength of "rasp." A good writer, according to Hall,
looks with hungry eyes and listens with greedy ears for
lively, engaging, powerful words.

Dictionaries help in this search. A thesaurus, which lists words that are similar in meaning, can be useful, but only to help us remember words, not to discover new ones. Replacing a word we know with one we have never used increases the chances for distorting what we mean to say. Use the thesaurus, then, to find the *right* word, the one you once knew but forgot when you needed it.

Of the standard pocketbook dictionaries, there are many. They all have the advantage of defining a word, but their definitions are so brief and limited that they increase the risk of your misusing the word. When it comes to dictionaries, the more information, the better. And when it comes to information, no dictionary can equal the *Oxford English Dictionary*. Robert Graves said it is the only indispensable book in a writer's library.

But it is not just its completeness that separates the OED from all the others; the OED also shows words in contexts. It tells the history of every word from its earliest appearance in print, and every new definition and shade of meaning is supported by a sentence in which the word is used. And who do you think wrote the sentences? Shakespeare, Donne, Milton, Austen, Hardy, Eliot—all our language's greatest writers.

The OED tells us why the word "critical" means something different today than it did when most of us were born and why, if we knew the original meaning of the word "key," we would blush every time we opened a door. The OED tells us why "nice" isn't a "nice" word and why before 1969 no one pronounced "defense" as "*de*-fense." Before 1969 it was always "de-*fense*." Coaches used to tell their players, "You people think defense is something that runs around the yard." The change in pronunciation killed that joke. So what happened in 1969? New York Knicks basketball fans had their first championship team. They were on television a lot that winter. People all over the country heard them shouting "*DE*-FENSE! *DE*-FENSE!"

It's all in the *Oxford English Dictionary*. So are three columns on the word "vegetable." "Vegetable" came into our language as an adjective in 1400. This is why Andrew Marvell could write that his "vegetable love" should grow "vaster than empires and more slow." He wasn't saying he was a "couch potato"; he wanted his love to be allowed to ripen slowly over a long period of time.

When did "vegetable" get to be a noun? In 1582. Between 1582 and today, there have been thirty-six different contexts and shades of meaning for the word "vegetable."

If you enjoy learning about words, your sensitivity to their sounds and meanings will increase every time you open the *Oxford English Dictionary*. And the more you learn about how words code our history and development as people, the more you will respect them, the more honestly you will use them, and the greater impact you will make them have on your readers.

—5—

MECHANICS

TOOLS FOR COMMUNICATION

> The difficulty is not to write but to write what you mean, not to affect your reader but to affect him precisely as you wish.
>
> —*Robert Louis Stevenson*

Many writers see the rules that determine spelling punctuation and grammar as a strait jacket insofar as these rules have only to do with what is correct and what is incorrect they are right the major purpose of these rules however is rhetorical they help us communicate more effectively they make it easier for our readers to understand exactly what we mean the way we make spaces between our words is just as important as the words themselves.

See where we'd be without punctuation? Imagine if we took out spelling and syntax as well.

We expect writing to be correct. We don't often praise it when it is, but we sure notice when it isn't. No matter how brilliant the insight or provocative the analysis, mistakes distract us. They make us question the credibility of the writer.

What's "correct" or "incorrect," however, is not the province of the office grammarian or any single guide to style. And the likes of William Safire and John Simon are the last people to be given the final word on this subject. In their honest attempts to save the language from instability and imprecision, they also hinder its growth. Their job, as evidenced from their books and articles, is to retard whatever enlivens and enriches the spoken language from enlivening and enriching the written language. Fortunately, theirs is a losing battle. It always has been and probably always will be. Thanks to the power and energy of the spoken word—the written word's experimental laboratory—we can now end our sentences in prepositions, split an occasional infinitive, choose not to distinguish between "who" and "whom" or "that" and "which," substitute "like" for "as," commit the sin of comma splicing, "begin a sentence with "and," and "but," and "because," follow the singular "none" with a plural verb ("None of you are wrong"), use "whose" instead of "which" when speaking about an inanimate object ("The house whose garden . . ."), and use a plural pronoun to include men and women when the subject is singular ("Every writer needs to demonstrate their ability").

Much of the tension that exists between our spoken and written prose stems from the time when America was a colony. The people then didn't want to weaken their ties with England. They wanted to hold on to her (or is it now "its"?) customs, traditions, conventions. One of the ways they did this was to maintain all the grammmatical rules they had brought over with them. Had they not, our spoken English would sound today more like the English that is spoken in England. On the other hand, now we can say that Marlon Brando's English is closer to the one Shakespeare spoke than Laurence Olivier's.

How can we resolve this conflict between the old and the new, the written and the spoken, the "correct" and the "incorrect"?

Be Yourself. The more you are yourself on paper, the more interesting, lively, and "correct" you will be. We speak in simple yet colorful ways. We also make ourselves easy to understand. If we write the same way, much of what we write will "correct" itself. Simple, clear, easy-to-understand sentences are not hard to punctuate. It's only when we get caught up in trying to sound like someone we're not that our writing gets complicated.

Assume a New Identity. After you've finished writing your rough draft, become a copy editor. You want to see what's on the paper now, not what's in your head. You want to see what you said, not what you wanted to say. The best way to do this is to put some time and distance between you and what you've written. Get a cup of coffee; go to lunch; head home for the day. The more time and distance you can put between what you've written and what you're going to edit, the more objective you'll be. Then, when you return, read through what you've written several times before focusing on the individual sentences and words. Sometimes errors have a way of revealing themselves when we're not so close to them.

After you've made sure everything has been set down just as you intended and you didn't leave anything out, go through your writing line by line, word by word, and comma by comma. Make sure you spelled all the words correctly and you caught all your typographical errors. Then, to double check, read your memo or letter or whatever backwards. Word by word. Sometimes, because we know what we've written, we tend to correct things unconsciously. We fill in a missing word or letter without realizing it. Reading backwards helps us discover these unconscious corrections. The important thing to remember as a copy editor, however, is not the sanctity of any rule but each individual sentence. If, when you read it out loud, the sentence sounds right, it most likely is right even if it may be mechanically incorrect. In these cases, what works best may be more important than someone else's idea of what's right or wrong.

The first four chapters of this book talk most about how to get ideas and how to develop them, style and structure, and how to write clear, lively, engaging, powerful prose. Many of the problems people have with spelling, punctuation, and grammar can be resolved naturally by prewriting, freewriting, and rewriting. You don't have to know a whole bunch of rules to write well. Of more importance is a sensitivity to words: how they sound and what they mean.

The best way to develop a sensitivity to words is to have something to say and to want to say it. Then the "rules," those conventions our readers expect to find when they pick up something we've written, will seem more like means than ends. They will be appreciated as the tools we need to lead our readers where we want them to go.

Fortunately, those who prewrite, freewrite, and rewrite make very few mechanical errors, usually not more than three or four. The problem, as noted in the writing centers at the City University of New York, is that they make the same mistakes over and over again. This chapter, then, continues our discussion on how to write with vigor and clarity, but it approaches the subject from a different angle: how to get out of the swamps we find ourselves repeatedly mired in and back on to the road of simple, direct prose.

SPELLING

> It's a damn poor mind that can think of only one way
> to spell a word.
>
> *—Andrew Jackson*

Of all the rules concerning mechanics, none is so tyrannical as spelling. In almost every single case, a word is either right or wrong. There are very few shades of gray. "Inquire" and "enquire" is one. Both words mean "to ask," and either spelling is acceptable, providing both spellings don't appear in the same piece of writing.

But the seemingly arbitrary decisions made regarding spelling wouldn't bother us so much if they were only consistent from one word to the next. Unfortunately, there are very few rules that some word hasn't found a way to break. And I'm not talking about the obvious ones, such as "i" before "e" except after "c." I'm talking about spellings of sounds like "sh." There are twelve different ways to spell "sh" in English. Here they are:

shoe	suspicion
sugar	nauseous
ocean	conscious
issue	chaperone
nation	mansion
pshaw	fuchsia

When George Bernard Shaw discovered this, he's reported to have said it made him think of another "sh" word. Shaw pointed out that if you followed the rules of spelling, you could spell the word "fish" this way: ghoti. Just take the "gh" sound as it appears in "enough," the "i" sound as it appears in "women," and the "sh" sounds as it appears in "fiction." There you have it: ghoti.

Then there are the words we've all developed blocks against. John Irving, an admitted poor speller, tells us he can never spell the word "strictly." He always spells it "strickly." In one five-year period, Irving looked up "strickly" fourteen times. In that same period, he looked up the word "ubiquitous" twenty times. Not only can he still not spell it, he can barely remember what it means.

And yet, in spite of how smart we are or how much we know, we are judged by our ability to spell. People lose confidence in what we have to say if our messages contain misspelled words. Oscar Wilde was joking about this perhaps unfair and certainly mistaken association between spelling and intelligence when he said, "A writer can tolerate anything but a misprint."

If you're a poor speller, you'll probably always be a poor speller. Sounding the word out, as you were taught in grammar school, goes only so far, and you've learned not to rely on your eyes. There are, however, some things you can do to cut down on the number of misspelled words that creep into your writing.

Develop a Dialogue with Your Dictionary. This is what John Irving does. Whenever he looks up a word, he puts a check next to that word in the dictionary's margin. If he looks up the word again, he puts another check. This makes him concentrate more on the word he's looked up and serves as a reminder if he comes across it while looking up another word. Most of the time, it works. In the cases of "strictly" and "ubiquitous," obviously, it hasn't. And it probably never will. At least for Irving.

But Irving also uses his search for the correct ways to spell words as an opportunity to expand his vocabulary. After he puts a check next to the word he's looked up, he looks at all the other words on the page. He finds one he doesn't know but would like to learn. Next to this word, he writes the date. Then he learns the word. He may not remember it very long—especially if he doesn't use it—but the date gives him some idea of how long it took him to forget it. He sees it as a game to make looking up words less tiresome and learn some new words at the same time.

Irving also suggests saying whatever new words you've learned before putting them in writing. Sometimes a dictionary's definition isn't as clear as it should be. Using a new word a few times in conversations with friends helps us to clarify and confirm its meaning. It also helps us spell better. By saying a new word we learn how to pronounce it, and pronunciation—sounding the word out—can lessen our chances of misspelling, provided, of course, that the word looks the way it sounds.

Stick to the Words You Speak. Ninety percent of all good writing consists of only 1,000 words. These are the words we speak every day. Rarely do we misspell a word that we say regularly. If we use in our writing only the words we speak, we'll greatly reduce our spelling errors.

Here are two lists of words. The words on the left are the kind we tend to speak; the ones on the right are what these words come out as whenever we pick up a pen or sit down in front of a typewriter. Notice the degree of spelling difficulty that separates them:

after	subsequent
agree	concur
begin	commence
happen	transpire
use	utilize

Sticking to the words we speak, it should be noted, works best when we pronounce these words correctly. Many people find themselves writing "nucular," for example, instead of "nuclear" because they say "new-kew-ler" instead of "new-klee-er." The same goes for "athelete" instead of "athlete," "Febuary" instead of "February," "libary" instead of "library," and "Wendsday" instead of "Wednesday." Then, of course, there are those who always spell some words correctly because they've taught themselves to pronounce the word as it is spelled: "mis*chie*vous," as in "chief's daughter," instead of "misschevus."

Keep a List of Your Most Frequently Misspelled Words. Even when you're developing a dialogue with your dictionary, looking up words can seem like a waste of time and energy, especially when you've looked up the word twenty times in the past five years. If you feel this way, keep a list of the words you love to misspell. This way you can check your spelling quickly and not feel discouraged by the collection of checks and dates you've been compiling in the margins of your dictionary. You may also wish to consider underlining the part of the word that gives you trouble.

Notice How Other People Spell. Notice not just the words you have trouble with, but new ones as well. Books, magazines, newspapers, even restaurant menus can help your spelling. Words like "environment," "separate," and "describe" are common troublemakers. If you tend to write "enviroment," "seperate," or "discribe," paying more attention to what you read can help. Truely. Did you notice, for example, that if you are in the habit of writing "resturant," you had an opportunity in this paragraph to see it spelled correctly? And did you notice I wrote "truely" when I should have written "truly"? If so, you're probably not as bad a speller as you think.

Make Friends with a Good Speller. Wilfred Stone tells us in *Prose Style* that there's only one rule for spelling: If you're not sure, look it up. But what if you are sure, and the word is still misspelled? Only someone else can find this kind of error. Ask a good speller to proofread your work. Add the words he or she finds to your list of most frequent misspellings. Before long you'll be finding most of these words yourself.

PUNCTUATION

I spent the whole morning putting in a comma; I spent the whole afternoon taking it out again.
                                             —*Oscar Wilde*

Until the eighteenth century, there were almost no rules for punctuation. The heavy influence of Latin had made the kinds of punctuation we use today unnecessary. It wasn't long, however, before people began marking the cadences that were then fashionable in less formal prose. Things quickly got out of hand. Pretty soon there were more than thirty different kinds of punctuation. Reading was like driving down a bad road. Curves, detours, potholes, and more kept demanding that readers reduce their speed or change directions.

The natural, faster cadences of the twentieth century call for a different approach. Today's readers, more often than not, are in a hurry. They want Interstate Prose. Of course, there are disadvantages to this kind of reading. Who, for example, wants to speedread a novel? But for absorbing the kind of information that doesn't require much reflection, freeway prose may be the way to go. One advantage of this faster prose—at least for the writer—is that it's made many of those thirty punctuation marks obsolete. They may pop up now and then but, for the most part, we don't use more than twelve.

That's the good news. The bad news is that one of those twelve gives us more trouble than all thirty combined: the comma. Depending on the book you read, there can be as many as a dozen uses for the comma. Fortunately, we need only one rule to handle them all: *When in doubt, leave 'em out.*

The Comma

Most of us know about five ways to use commas. Those ways that you are absolutely sure of, continue to use. Forget about the rest. You didn't learn them in grammar school; you didn't learn them in high school; you didn't learn them in college or professional school or on the job. You've probably built up such a block of anxiety about the comma uses you don't know, you'll probably never learn them. So forget about them. Even the most unreasonable grammarian can find all kinds of reasons why you may have left a comma out of a sentence, but put one in where it doesn't belong and it is wrong every single time. Here, simply stated, are the most common uses of the comma.

Use a Comma to Indicate a Pause if You Were Reading Out Loud. This is the oldest comma use, and we'd all be a lot better off if it had remained the only one. The other uses have made this one true only up to a point. Now there are places in our writing where commas are necessary even though we would not pause there. *The New Yorker* magazine, for example, loves commas. Rarely do its editors miss an opportunity to put a comma rule into practice:

> During the morning, more or less as Toperih-peri had predicted, the Turkana, avoiding the pass, which, as To-perih-peri could have told them, was sure to be guarded, had entered the district between Morukore and Kalapata and, turning north instead of south, raided a neighborhood on the plain.

None of these comma placements is incorrect, but, to quote H. W. Fowler, "Any one who finds himself putting down several commas close to one another should reflect that he is making himself disagreeable and question whether it is necessary."

Use Commas to Separate Items in a Series. "Your review will be read by the committee, the board, and the president." Some grammarians would say that the comma in front of "and" is unnecessary, and they would be right. One of the original functions of the comma was to take the place of "and." Without commas, some people would have to be tall and dark and handsome. But this question of the comma before "and" is really one of fashion. Some years it is in; others it is out. Right now it is in to leave the comma out. The comma will return, however, when enough pro-comma people complain loud enough about a sentence like "He touched first, second and third." Any reader who didn't know something about baseball might think this player could somehow touch second and third at the same time. The logic of this argument notwithstanding, journalists always leave the comma out for a reason that has nothing to do with language: Leaving the comma out saves space.

Sometimes you can have a list of adjectives that don't require commas. Three blind mice, for example. The general rule here is that if you can say the word "and" between each adjective in the series, you need a comma; if saying "and" doesn't sound right, leave the comma out. Unless, of course, the sentence looks odd with the commas in, as in "The three blind mice were short, gray, and fast." For purposes of symmetry and length, you could probably break the "and" rule here without too much fearing reprisal.

Use a Comma to Set off an Introductory Phrase. This is a popular use of the comma: "When Aunt Helen and Uncle Dick arrive, the fun begins." But what happens if the opening phrase is a short one? "When Aunt Helen arrives the fun begins," for example. Or "In 1960 Helen drove with us to California."

Some people, like the editors at *The New Yorker*, put a comma in after every introductory anything regardless of how short it is. Others use commas only after long introductory phrases and clauses. Whichever "rule" you choose, be consistent. In borderline cases, let your ears decide. You wouldn't want to write, for example, "Before testing the reactor was fired." If you're still not sure, rewrite the sentence so the question of commas is no longer an issue: "The reactor was fired before it had been tested."

Use a Comma to Separate Two Sentences That Are Joined by "and," "or," "nor," "for," or "but." In these cases, the comma is placed just before the word joining the sentences: "The committee discussed the problem for hours, but no one could come up with a solution." If the two sentences are short, however, you may wish for reasons of pace or rhythm to leave the comma out: "The wine was old but that didn't stop us from drinking it."

Use Commas to Set Off Appositives. Appositives are words that clarify the words in front of them: "My friend, Jerry, called me this morning." Once again, however, you may wish to leave these commas out for reasons that are more important than being correct. What if the call were urgent and you wanted to give the reader a sense of that urgency in your sentence? In this case, "My friend Jerry called me" works better without the commas.

Use Commas to Set Off Phrases That Limit or Clarify Their Subjects. These phrases are sort of like big appositives. Sometimes they can even amount to clauses. The way to identify them is to see if the sentence can stand without them: "The Pope, who surrounded himself with huge fires, escaped the plague." "The Pope escaped the plague" could stand alone, but "who surrounded himself with huge fires" is important because it explains how the Pope survived. These phrases or clauses that tell us something about their subjects need to be separated from the rest of the sentence by commas.

Use Commas to Separate Quotations from the Rest of the Sentence. E. B. White tells us, "Vigorous writing is concise. A sentence should contain no unnecessary words, a paragraph no unnecessary sentences, for the same reason that a drawing should have no unnecessary lines or a machine no unnecessary parts." A sentence shouldn't have any unnecessary commas either, but as a signal to the reader that a quotation is coming, the comma is considered indispensible by most grammarians. Sometimes it can be replaced by a colon (:) if we want the reader to know that what follows is important, but you never need a comma if your quotation is a part of your sentence: "William Goldman told me 'the key to being a successful writer is not talent; it's discipline.' " In every other case, however, use a comma to separate your quotation from the other words in the sentence:

Pablo Neruda writes, "All paths lead to the same goal: to convey to others what we are."

"There is no greatness," Leo Tolstoi tells us, "where there is not simplicity, goodness, and truth."

"Being a writer means having to prove your talent to people who have none," said Joseph Joubert.

"There is nothing to writing," Red Smith once wrote. "All you do is sit down at a typewriter and open a vein."

Use Commas to Separate Words from Their Appendages. Many of these uses are basic:

Brooklyn, New York, is . . .

On August 14, 1914, Europe . . .

Trinity College, Dublin, houses . . .

There are, as you may have guessed, some exceptions. "Jr.," "Inc.," and academic degrees don't require commas after them, though there are some cases—this sentence for example—where they are helpful. Here are some cases where they are unnecessary:

J. B. Bessinger, Jr. lectures . . .

Helene Hinis, Ph.D. writes . . .

Trentex, Inc. offers . . .

A few appendages don't require any commas at all:

Richard III rode into . . .

7:45 P.M. marks . . .

The fourth century B.C. is . . .

Generally speaking, short sentences require fewer commas than long sentences. If we write the kinds of sentences we speak, we aren't going to need many commas. Most of the time we can leave them out and still be correct. The problem most writers have with commas, however, is that if they go a few sentences without using one, they start shaking them over their prose as if they were salt.

Here are some sentences that either don't need or shouldn't have any commas in them:

Of course, I represent the company.

After I left, he called the office.

I went to meet Bruce, and Philip.

Bobby sells, tires, mufflers, and headlights.

A writer, who wants to be successful, has to write, every day.

The Comma Splice. Now for the biggest comma error/non-error of them all. In a comma splice, a comma is made to do the work of a period. Or to put it another way, in a comma splice, two sentences are separated not by a period, but by a comma. What's confusing about comma splice errors is that the reader is led to believe that two separate ideas are connected (spliced) when they are not:

Live all you can, it's a mistake not to.

Never play another person's game, play your own.

Peace cannot be kept by force, peace can only be kept by understanding.

The commas in these sentences tell us we are reading one continuous idea, but we see as we read past each comma that there are really two ideas. Each of these ideas should be a separate sentence. Or joined in some other way. There are several ways these sentences could have been written to avoid the comma splice errors.

They could have been joined by a semicolon:

Live all you can; it's a mistake not to.

They could have been joined by a comma and a conjunction:

Never play another person's game, but play your own.

They could have been made into one sentence with one clause depending on the other:

When peace cannot be kept by understanding, it cannot be kept by force.

Now here's the kicker. Every one of those sentences containing comma splice errors is also correct as it is. Remember when I said in the introduction that every rule can be broken? John Fowles writes, "Follow the accident, fear the fixed plan—that is the rule." That's three separate sentences in one, but who's going to tell John Fowles he's a poor writer? The point, as always, is use what works best. For Fowles, it was this construction.

To determine whether you want to separate your ideas with a comma, a period, a semicolon, a comma and a conjunction, or a dash, read your sentences out loud. Each solution will give your sentence a slightly different tone or meaning. By reading the sentence out loud, you can best determine the most appropriate and effective structure.

Here are some more comma splice–ridden sentences from

two of our most respected writers. See if any "correct" versions improve on what they have to say:

> People do not deserve to have good writing, they are so pleased with bad.
>
> —Ralph Waldo Emerson

> Whatever our theme in writing, it is old and tried. Whatever our place, it has been visited by the stranger, it will never be new again. It is only the vision that can be new; but that is enough.
>
> —Eudora Welty

The Colon

A colon can sometimes take the place of a comma. When it does, the writer is telling us: Hey! What's coming right after this colon is very important, so pay attention.

> Red Smith once wrote: "There is nothing to writing. All you do is sit down at a typewriter and open a vein."

In the preceding example, a comma could appear after "wrote," but this writer chose a colon because she wanted to emphasize the importance of the quotation.

Sometimes a writer will capitalize the first word after the colon to further emphasize the importance of the message.

> The chief soon discovered the cause of the fire: Arson.

In addition to important quotations and important words, colons can introduce lists.

> The student narrowed his reading list to three authors: Nathaniel Hawthorne, Herman Melville, and Mark Twain.

The most common use of the colon for business and professional people, however, is in the salutations of their letters.

Dear Ms. Hemingway:

Dear Michael:

Joseph:

The rarest use of the colon is to place it between two independent clauses;

Five minutes seemed like a week and a half: Hubert had never been late before.

In this case, the colon takes the place of a semicolon, but it gives the sentence a meaning it wouldn't have with a semicolon. The colon implies that there is more than just a connection between the two clauses; it implies that the second clause is derived from the first. This particular use of the colon is so rare, however, that most editors would change the colon to a period.

The Semicolon

The semicolon rates high on most people's list of hated punctuation marks because it is so misunderstood. Like so many heavies in movies from the 1930s, however, there really is a nice guy underneath.

The semicolon, basically, joins two sentences. It takes the place of the period that separates them or the comma and conjunction that may join them. In other words, if you want to avoid semicolons, use a period. If, however, you want a pause that's shorter than a period but still longer than a comma, the semicolon is your mark. But don't try to replace a comma with it unless you're John Fowles or Margaret Atwood or you're writing for someone who reads

books written by people like John Fowles or Margaret Atwood. Except in these cases, the only time a semicolon can
stand in for a comma is when the comma works with a
conjunction ("and," "but," "or," "nor") to join two sentences
together. In these cases both the comma *and* the conjunction have to come out. For example, you have two sentences
already joined by a comma and the conjunction "and":

John hit the ball, and he ran to first.

You want to speed up the action. Take out the comma and
the conjunction; replace them with a semicolon:

John hit the ball; he ran to first.

To turn the speed up even higher, replace the semicolon
with a comma:

John hit the ball, he ran to first.

But beware: Traditional grammarians react strongly to this.
One editor told me it was like getting buried with your fly
open. Another said the only worse mistake was not using
any punctuation at all. Nevertheless, many of our language's best writers are doing it, and they're the ones who
set the pace for the rest of us to follow.

The Apostrophe

The apostrophe is a little mark that seems to cause a lot
of confusion when we write but is almost always clear when
we read. Basically there are two rules, two fashions, and
two problems in apostrophedom. The two rules are as follows:

1. To show ownership, add an apostrophe and an "s"
to singular nouns:

the boy's bag

the girl's lunch

the school's classrooms

2. If the noun is plural, add only the apostrophe to show ownership:

the boys' bag (All the boys own one bag.)

the girls' lunches (All the lunches are owned by all the girls.)

the schools' classrooms (More than one school owns all the classrooms.)

The two fashions are:

1. If the singular noun ends in an "s," add either an apostrophe or an apostrophe and an "s." Both "Thomas' job" and "Thomas's job" are correct, though the current trend favors using just the apostrophe: "Thomas' job."

2. For singular nouns ending in "x" or "z," most people use the apostrophe and the "s": "Fritz's campaign was still a long way from Marx's thinking."

And the two problems are:

1. Add apostrophe and an "s" to plural nouns not ending in "s":

The men's room

Women's rights

The people's struggle

2. Be careful when using an apostrophe to show something is plural. Which is correct: "Four Ph.D.s work for the

company" or "Four Ph.D.'s work for the company"? In this case, the apostrophe doesn't seem to matter; we know that there's more than one Ph.D. But what about "She received two Cs on her report card" or "Reggie Jackson is now stirring drinks for the Oakland As"? What are the "do's" and "don'ts" here?

You have to decide each case individually. Forget about trying to find a rule to apply to even most situations. Ask instead, what helps my reader the best? Obviously "do's" is better than "dos" and "A's" is more effective than "As." In cases where the "'s" doesn't matter, you may wish to leave out the apostrophe—especially if your reader might think those four Ph.D.'s own something.

The Hyphen

Once a rage in the nineteenth century—only roller skating was said to be more widespread—hyphens are enjoying a comeback. And for good reason. There's a big difference between "four foot lights" and "four-foot lights." Hyphens can be used in a variety of ways.

Joining Two Adjectives Before a Noun.

Coney Island has a mile-long beach.

The lifeguards wear carrot-orange uniforms.

If the adjectives come after the word they modify, however, a hyphen isn't necessary:

The beach at Coney Island is a mile long.

The lifeguards' uniforms are carrot orange.

The danger in combining words with hyphens is a tendency to string out too many of these newly formed compound words. In some cases, they give the appearance of wash on a line:

> The carrot-orange, green-striped, brief-bottomed lifeguard uniforms . . .

Avoiding Ambiguity. "Re-creation" needs a hyphen to prevent confusion with "recreation." "Co-operate" doesn't need a hyphen. To be sure, check your dictionary.

Preventing Awkward Spelling. Hyphens help us avoid writing words such as "exwife" and "tshirt." Again, check your dictionary when you're not sure.

Breaking Words at the Right-Hand Margin. Dictionaries use bullets (•) to indicate the syllables where a word may be divided (mis•ap•pre•hend). The way we pronounce a word may lead us to break it where we *think* the syllables fall: "min-or," for example, instead of "mi-nor" or "per-suas-ion" instead of "per-sua-sion." When it comes to breaking words, there are no alternatives. Words must be divided where the dictionary says they must be divided. This is an aid to pronunciation and, therefore, to reading.

Quotation Marks. Quotation marks can be used to emphasize a word or cite an example, but their main functions are two:

1. *To show what someone said.* Georg Christoph Lichtenberg tells us, "A book is a mirror; if an ass peers into it, you can't expect an apostle to peer out."

2. *To identify the title of a short story, poem, article, chapter in a book, one-act play, or any other short pieces of writing.* Titles of longer works—books, plays, movies, newspapers, and magazines—are commonly underlined, indicating italic letters (some stylebooks prefer non-italic capital letters). Some word processors and computer systems can produce italics.

In "Writers on Writing," a chapter in his book *Writing for Your Readers*, Donald Murray shares with us these words by Willa Cather: "It takes a great deal of experience to become natural."

The major trouble with quotation marks comes when we begin mixing them with periods, commas, and question marks. This poses no problems for a sentence such as:

John asked, "What did he say?"

But if the speaker asks a question about the words in the quotation, the question mark should go outside of the quotation marks:

Did the boss say, "I want that report by Monday"?

Generally speaking, periods and commas go inside the quotation marks, while colons and semicolons go outside of them. Question marks depend on the situation, and common sense is the most reliable source for determining what is correct.

The Dash

Because it speeds the reader along, the dash has virtually replaced the colon (:) and parentheses ( ). An attention-getting device, it also has the look of an arrow pointing our way to an important part of the sentence. And when you consider the uses of the colon—to set off a list or clarify a point—the dash's high visibility is warranted. Parentheses offer the writer high visibility, but they slow the reader down. And whereas parentheses look somewhat formal, the dash gives the impression of speech.

Here's an example of a dash replacing a colon:

Three people won promotions last week—Jim, Martha, and Joan.

And one of a dash replacing parentheses:

Many readers—unless they favor scholarly journals—welcome the dash.

The dash can also be used to show a slight hesitation—as in an aside or afterthought—before following through with the rest of the sentence. The danger with dashes, however, is that—because of their popularity—people tend to use them as substitutes for other forms of punctuation—like commas and periods (as I just did). There's nothing wrong with doing this—at least not yet—but too many substitutions weaken the dash—as the sentences in this paragraph demonstrate—as well as rob the other punctuation marks of their meaning and uses.

Punctuation marks were created to make life easier. Unlike the rules of spelling, there is not much that is illogical about them. And if they cause more problems because they are less fixed than spelling rules, they also provide more opportunities. In fact, the more ways we can think of to use a particular punctuation mark, the more flexibility it has.

This, of course, doesn't mean that anything goes. In fact, if there's one place where we may want to play conservatively, it is in our use of punctuation. The purpose of punctuation is to help our readers understand what we're trying to say. Straying too far from the familiar runs the risk of having our message lost. So stick to the conventional unless it sounds affected or just doesn't work for what you have in mind. It's the least our readers expect and frees us to be more creative elsewhere.

SYNTAX

When I stepped from hard manual work to writing,
I just stepped from one kind of hard work to another.
—Sean O'Casey

Syntax is the way we arrange our words when we write or speak. Some arrangements work better than others; some arrangements don't work at all.

There are two approaches to the study of syntax: the traditional and the structural. The traditional approach, based mostly on Latin rules applied to English, is the one most of us are familiar with. It works, but only up to a point. Not all the rules can be remembered, and many of them can't be applied to every situation. The structural approach, on the other hand, focuses on the way the simplest English sentences are put together. From these simple sentences come our more complex structures. It is these structures in our language, rather than the individual words, that syntax is concerned with.

If you are a native speaker of English, you know what you need to structure a sentence. You've been doing it all your life. As long as you write as you speak, you'll almost always arrange your words in simple, clear, easy-to-understand ways.

There are a few times, however, when we need some help. No single person has difficulty with all of the syntax problems that follow. Most of us struggle with only one or two. Nevertheless, syntactic errors are difficult to spot in our own writing, and we tend to repeat them frequently.

After you discover the error or two that you make, save one proofreading of your writing for syntax. Then, when you have someone else look at your work, ask him or her to keep a special lookout for the mistakes you're most likely to make.

Subject–Verb Agreement

We all know that singular subjects take singular verbs, but sometimes we place our verbs so far away from our subjects that, without realizing it, we match our verbs with some other word in the sentence. For example:

> Bob's working *habits*, like his way of playing baseball, *is* marked by patience and seizing opportunities.

If I had gone from "habits" right into saying what characterizes them, I would certainly have matched the verb's number with the subject's. Because I inserted "like his way of playing baseball," however, "baseball" was the last word I had in mind before I wrote down our verb. And because "baseball" was the last word in mind, I *naturally*, perhaps even unconsciously, matched the verb with it rather than with the subject, "habits."

What irritates us about agreement problems of this kind is that we all know better. We all know that our subjects and verbs have to match, and what's worse, we know how to match them. Unfortunately, we're sometimes distracted by other words in the sentence and match our verbs with them instead of the words they should be matched with.

Here are two more examples of verb agreement errors:

> An *agenda* for including these recent developments *remain* to be discussed.

The *newspaper* with the best reporters *do* the best job.

Seeing the errors in other people's ways is easy. Nevertheless, some words continue to trouble us. Words like "each," "anyone," "anybody," "no one," "nobody," "everyone," "everybody," "someone," and "somebody." These words all require *singular* verbs:

Each *has* to . . .

Anyone *is* allowed to . . .

Someone *is* needed to . . .

Everyone *is* responsible for . . .

Everybody *has* the right to . . .

Nouns joined by "and," however, require a plural verb:

John *and* Mary arrive on Tuesday.

The few exceptions to this rule are mostly idiomatic:

Peanut butter and jelly *is* a sure hit.

Rock 'n' roll *is* here to stay.

In all these cases, your ear is the best judge for determining the most effective syntax.

Nouns joined by "or" or "nor" use singular verbs if all the nouns are singular, plural verbs if the nouns are plural:

Either IBM or Macintosh *has* to back down.

Neither businessmen nor politicians *want* war.

When one noun is singular and the other is plural, the verb agrees in number with the closest noun.

Noun and Pronoun Agreement

The problem here stems from the same root as verb agreement: too many words between the words we are matching. Only here the problem is compounded by the fact that we don't always know the correct way to match our pronouns with the nouns they refer to. The rule is simple: Make pronouns and nouns agree in number and gender. It's the application that's confusing. And that confusion has increased with the raised feminine consciousness. Writing "his or her" or "his/her" every time you want to make these pronouns agree with a singular noun can irritate your reader, and though the *Oxford English Dictionary* tells us it is now correct to use "their" where both sexes are concerned, many people still regard it as wrong.

What, for example, would you do with this sentence:

Each (have, has) a computer of (his, her, their) own.

Because "each" is singular, it requires the singular verb "has." But which pronoun shall we choose? "His" pleases the traditionalists, "his or her" gives each sex its due but can appear graceless if repeated too often, and while "their" is less distracting than "his or her" it doesn't agree with "each." In short, every one of these pronouns can be "right" or "wrong" depending on whom you ask.

In matters of gender, each writer has to decide for him- or herself (see pages 102–105). In all other cases, nouns and pronouns must agree in number. If the noun is singular, the pronoun must be singular; if the noun is plural, the pronoun must be plural.

This rule is clear in a sentence such as "One of the boys

forgot his lunch," where "his" refers to "one" rather than "boys," but what about these sentences?

The plan was for everyone on the committee to use (his, her, their) records.

Either the president or the vice-president missed (his call their call).

Most of the time you can solve this problem by substituting the article—"the," "a," or "an"—for the pronoun:

The plan was for everyone on the committee to use *the* records.

Either the president or the vice-president missed *a* call.

This eliminates the sexist "his," the awkward "his or her," and the incorrect or at least informal "their."

Some words like "group," "committee," and "board" are called collective nouns because they are "singular" words that refer to collections of people. Whether you use a singular or plural verb or pronoun, however, depends on whether you're referring to the whole group or its individual members. Say, for example, you write:

The board took the elevator to its office.

This means all the members of the board went together to the office where the board meets. On the other hand, you might write:

The board took the elevator to their offices.

Now you're saying the board members went to their individual offices. Both sentences are correct; the pronouns make it clear what you mean. Here are some examples where the pronouns and collective nouns are mismatched:

The board went to its separate offices.

The committee voted to disband themselves.

The group decided to share their results.

Other rules involving pronoun agreement include: Two or more nouns joined by "and" always take a plural pronoun:

When Mary and John reported for work, *they* . . .

When a pronoun refers to nouns joined by "or," "nor," "either . . . or," or "neither . . . nor," and one of the nouns is plural, make the pronoun match the noun it's closest to:

Neither Harry nor the Hendersons remembered *their* luggage.

These sentences also read better if the second of the two nouns and the matching pronoun are plural. Finally, beware of using a pronoun that could refer to more than one noun:

When Mary had to let Linda go, she was disappointed.

Misplaced Modifiers

Rarely do we write an adjective that doesn't come right before or right after the noun we want to describe. For some reason, however, we don't insist on the same proximity for our adjective phrases and clauses. We seem to think we can place them anywhere and our readers will know what we mean. Frequently readers do understand—

they misplace their modifiers too—but there is no syn-
tactical error that brings a smile to a reader's face sooner
or makes a writer look more foolish.

Consider these misplaced modifiers:

Old and rusted, I got the car cheap.

No doubt the car was in better shape than the buyer.

On reaching the age of thirty, his parents kicked him out
of the house.

How could two thirty-year-old parents do something like
that?

A complete fool, his employees got rid of him.

Not very bright employees.

Hopefully, this project will be completed in time.

The project hopes, but it doesn't do much about getting
itself done.

The problem with misplaced modifiers is that they create
ambiguity. Many times our readers can't tell what we really
mean. Even when our message isn't distorted, however,
misplaced modifiers can give the impression we're lazy or
don't care about what we write.

And yet these misreferences are so easy to correct:

The old and rusted car was cheap.

His employer got rid of him because he was a complete
fool.

I hope the project will be completed on time.

If only they were so easy to find! Take a break before tackling your final revision. Try to see through the eyes of an editor what you've written. Read your prose out loud and listen to what your ears tell you. If it doesn't sound right to you, it won't sound right to others. In fact, listening to what you've written is the most dependable way to catch agreement and modifier errors.

Then give your writing to someone else to read. The better the job you've done editing, the less work your proofreader will have to do. And the less work your proofreader does, the more willing he or she will be to read other things you've written.

FOUR STEPS TO ELIMINATE MECHANICAL ERRORS

> You can be a little ungrammatical if you come from the right part of the country.
> —*Robert Frost*

Write the Way You Talk. We speak in simple, clear, easy-to-understand sentences. If we write as closely as possible to the way we speak, we're going to make fewer mechanical errors. It's that simple. And that complicated. Many people have trouble breaking through the barrier that keeps them writing the way they think writing ought to be. Freewriting (see pages 27–39) helps us crash through that barrier. It frees us from the burden of carrying in our prose everyone else's preconceived ideas about what constitutes good writing. It enables us to develop our own natural writing styles.

Proofread Out Loud. We rely too much on our eyes, which miss a lot because they work so closely with our brains. They frequently see what isn't there and unconsciously correct what is. In short, they have a hard time changing their focus from what's in our heads to what's on the page. Our ears, on the other hand, have been listening to words for years. Many more words than our eyes have seen. Our ears know what sounds right and what doesn't. Listen to them. Except for catching spelling errors, they do almost everything else better than our eyes.

Ask Someone Else to Proofread Your Work. Someone whose intelligence you respect. Someone you know to be a good writer. If your office has a self-proclaimed grammarian who rubs everyone the wrong way, you don't have to look any farther. Even if this person is not a tactful critic, he or she has knowledge and can help you.

When a piece of writing has been edited and returned, make a list of all the mistakes. Repeat this process at least a half-dozen times. Every time you receive a corrected memo or letter, add your errors to the list. And don't just add the new errors; write them all down each time. Pretty soon you'll notice a pattern developing. The same mistakes keep reappearing. If you've written in your own voice and proof-read out loud, you almost certainly won't be making more than three errors. But you will be repeating those three.

Once you've identified your most common errors, find out how to correct them (the solution is likely to be found in the "Mechanics" section of this book). If one of your errors isn't among the most common, simply consult a book devoted solely to grammar. Once you've learned how to correct your mistakes, all you have to do is keep a special eye and ear out for them. Perhaps even devote one read-through of whatever you write just for those few likely errors.

Ask Yourself: Does It Work? Sometimes you won't agree with your proofreader's suggestions. You may want a third opinion. If another proofreader agrees with the first, you probably should listen. If, however, you feel strongly about what you've written, if you feel it accurately conveys what you want to say and will make your reader feel the way you want him or her to feel, then leave it alone. You are ultimately responsible for your own work. If you do what someone else tells you and the suggestions don't work, you'll kick yourself for not having followed your own sense of what worked best. If, on the other hand, you fail, you can find some comfort in your sense of integrity. At least you did what you thought was best and didn't try to be somebody you're not.

Fortunately, we rarely come across this sort of problem. Highly motivated writers—that is, writers who have something to say and want to say it—believe, have confidence in, and follow their intuition.

──6──

*B*USINESS WRITING

WRITING THAT MEANS BUSINESS

> Your writing is both good and original; but the part
> that is good is not original, and the part that is original
> is not good.
>
> —*Samuel Johnson*

Most business writing is dull—not in the sense of what we
say, but how we say it. We sound as if we've all been plugged
into the same machine.

Just because we work for institutions doesn't mean we
have to sound like them. Effective communication doesn't
mean using phrases like "prioritized evaluative procedures" or "modified departmental agenda." It means remembering that people identify with people, and in an
increasingly impersonal age, they are looking for human
contact. Those who give it to them win customers, establish
friendships, and yes, even make more money.

Here's an example of the kind of talk we create in our
flawed attempts to be taken seriously:

With regard to your claim (Acct. #9-4352), a copy of
the letter received in this office has been enclosed for

your perusal. Had there been a claim that was disallowed and with which payment was withheld by the debtor, the bill might have been closed, but since no pro was mentioned, the claim we referred to your office for collection, and which is referred to on the bill, is still liable for payment.

Why do we write this way? We'd never speak this way, and we wouldn't want to do business with anyone who did. Is trying to cover up our supposed inability to write clearly worth the time and effort it takes to create this kind of prose? Or have we somehow come to believe that a simple style reflects a simple mind?

The truth is that if we can talk clearly we can write clearly, and a muddled style reflects a muddled mind. Or one that is too dumb, too lazy, or too afraid to organize its thoughts and present them in a clear, direct, easy-to-understand way. The truth is that it's a lot tougher to make complex thoughts understandable than it is to make them more confusing. But there's no reason to make simple thoughts unintelligible.

Even when our message is clear, we tend to cloak it in something stuffy or pompous:

Pursuant to your query on the telephone this morning, please be advised that we no longer have in stock an original copy of the article you requested. A photocopy of the original copy is herewith enclosed.

If any further assistance is required, please do not hesitate to address your future correspondence directly to this office.

This is the old-fashioned way. Today's business letter—like the best writing of all times—is understandable without being condescending. It's also more personal than it's ever been. Take, for example, this rewrite:

I'm sorry we can't send you a copy of the article you requested. It is out of print. I am, however, enclosing a photocopy.

Please let me know if I can be of any further help.

Not only is the letter less stuffy, it is more concise and easy to read. It could, however, be more personal. Just wishing the reader good luck on his or her project or saying something about the article would have shown some interest in the reader as a person. As it is, the letter comes across as efficient but somewhat detached and almost all "I," "I," "I."

What we write is often the only chance we'll have to present ourselves to someone whose business we want. If what we say is pompous or unclear or impersonal, our readers are going to see us that way too. To avoid sending this kind of correspondence, ask yourself:

What do I sound like to others?

How will my readers take what I have written?

Would I want to meet with someone who writes like me?

Developing the kind of style that encourages people to want to meet with us is easier said than done. First of all, it's hard to separate ourselves from who we've become in our letters. And second, many businesses seem to equate unintelligible, dehumanized prose with professionalism.

Typical of the sentences we find in these "professional" letters, however, are gems like these:

Profits on imports partly compensate for the current burden on the manufacturing side.

Among the additional functional enhancements of the support program are dynamic reconfigurations and inter-systems communications.

The system was delivered with functionality.

This "Say what?" kind of language is no fun for the reader and can't possibly bring much joy to the writer either. Nevertheless, we've been taught to write this way, and few people are willing to risk their jobs trying to make businesses human.

There is a way to humanize your writing, however, and still maintain the kind of professional tone our companies expect of us. That is by writing in your own natural voice. But not the one that you would use when speaking to your friends or parents or children. If you are writing to someone who is the equivalent of a colleague or a peer, write in the same voice you would use when speaking to a colleague or peer. If you write to someone who is the equivalent of a boss or supervisor, write in the voice you use when speaking to your boss or supervisor. This way, you'll always be able to write naturally and, at the same time, maintain the standard level of English we've come to expect in a professional business letter.

MEMOS

> Writers are like baseball pitchers. Both have their moments. The intervals are the tough things.
>
> —*Robert Frost*

We use memos to communicate with others in our company. Every time we write one, we're given a chance to make others think well of us. And not just the people we've addressed them to. Memos that lie around the office or become part of a permanent record can be read by supervisors, chief executives, auditors, investigators, even people who have nothing better to do than read other people's memos.

Because of the wide range of people who may read our memos, it's important that their meanings be clear. Some of our readers may not know the same buzz words that we know; others may lack our knowledge. For this reason, it is usually a good idea to let our intended reader know exactly what our message is about. This doesn't mean we have to write the history behind every memo we write; rather, we want to make it clear to any reader exactly what matters we are talking about.

The way that we talk about these matters is crucial to our success. We can show our knowledge, character, creativity, and ability to articulate our ideas on paper or we can make another contribution to the bland file. Wouldn't it be best to write the kinds of memos that establish you as one of the few people in the company whose messages are always a pleasure to receive? Wouldn't it be great to be known as a writer of simple, clear, easy-to-understand prose? Wouldn't it be even better to be known as personable, lively, and engaging, as well as informative?

Here's how. Before writing any memo, ask yourself four questions.

Is This Memo Necessary? One of the secrets to writing effective memos is limiting yourself as much as possible to memos that count. Consider also that memos take time and energy to write: Would it be just as effective to telephone or go see the person? In many cases, the more personal, less formal speaking approach may be best. There are, after all, some disadvantages to memos. They're not easy to write, for one thing. They can't adjust to a reader's reaction the way a speaker adjusts to a listener's. Writing takes more time than speaking. And we can't change what we've written once we've sent it out. On the other hand, memos force us to articulate our thoughts. Getting our thoughts down on paper helps us make sure we know what we're talking about. And saying what we mean helps eliminate hearsay and rumors.

Memos also have a way of encouraging others to act. People may be able to avoid running into us or forget what we said on the phone, but they have a harder time ignoring something that's staring up at them from the desk. They know the only way to get rid of that memo is to act on it.

Memos, furthermore, may save time in the long run. They're not as easy as talking on the phone, but they enable us to reach any number of people almost simultaneously. We don't have to repeat ourselves, and, if our messages are well written, our readers don't have to telephone us to ask what we meant.

Finally, memos make good public relations agents. They get our name seen, they make sure we get credit for our ideas, and they free us to come up with other brilliant ideas.

In spite of these advantages, however, in a poll taken by Robert Half International the majority of our country's top executives complained that most memos are too long, too self-serving, sent to too many people, and written by people who write too many of them. The average executive, according to the poll, spends the equivalent of one month a year reading and writing unnecessary memos.

Who Am I Writing To? Who, specifically, is this person? How does he or she think, talk, and feel? What are his or her prejudices? What does he or she know? Need to know? Want to know?

In *The Million Dollar Memo* Cheryl Reimold tells us that the word "communicate" means a lot more than "inform." Sometimes we think because we've informed our readers of the facts, we've communicated those facts effectively. Then we wonder why we didn't get the response we wanted.

A good communicator, according to Reimold, tries to discover and answer as many of the reader's *human* needs as possible. A good communicator knows these are just as important as any facts. Moreover, people respond to this approach by trying to meet the communicator's needs.

What are these human needs? Reimold tells us the most

important ones are those that are beyond money or material things: companionship, approval, job satisfaction, mental stimulation, and increased learning.

Companionship. "Companion" comes from the Latin roots "com-," meaning "with," and "pan," meaning "bread." A companion is someone close enough to you to "have bread with." If we can make our readers feel as if they are our companions in work rather than mere functionaries, they're going to pay more attention and respond better to what we have to say. In other words, the language and tone of voice we use when speaking to a friend or close associate will go a longer way than any impersonal notice or computational buzz.

Approval. Approval has been a big issue with most of us since we were children. Respect your readers and show them that you value their efforts and they will work harder and longer to please you.

Job Satisfaction. Readers like to feel what they're doing is important. If you can, show your readers how your memos will help them in their work, as well as help you in yours. This also shows that you care and reinforces the feeling that they are special. Or at least human.

Mental Stimulation. Try to write memos that interest your readers. Share your feelings about what excites you in a way that encourages them to think about what you have to say. Give your readers the information they need to be mentally and emotionally involved in what you want them to do.

Increased Learning. People enjoy learning about things that affect them. Tell them why something has to be done a certain way. If they see another way but feel they can't talk about it with you or haven't been given enough information to see why their way won't work, they're going to think you're the one who is limited and they'll lose respect for you. They also won't do their job as well.

The more we know about our readers, the more ways we'll have of influencing them. The more we use these ways to "communicate" rather than "inform," the more effective our memos will be.

This doesn't mean we should be insincere or manipulative, however. It means we should write the way we would like to be written to: with respect, appreciation, and consideration.

What Do I Want to Say? Most of us know what we want to say when we write a memo, but you'd be surprised how often we don't say specifically what we mean or what we want our readers to do. Have you ever written a memo, for example, that ended with "Please advise," and when the reader responded, you got only some of the information you needed? You were lucky.

Say *specifically* what you want your readers to do and give them whatever they need to do it the way you want it done. To help your readers understand your memos better, ask the following questions:

- How much does the reader know about this subject?
- Are there any alternatives that might come to the reader's mind that would result in something I don't want?
- What questions might the reader ask?
- Can there be any mistake about my conclusions, solutions, and directions?

When Do I Want It Done? Have you ever asked for a reply "at your earliest convenience" and never received a response? Or when the reply came, so much time had passed you had a hard time remembering why you had written to the person in the first place?

Or have you ever written to somebody that you'd call next week about a certain matter, and when you called on Thursday afternoon, the person said, "I didn't think you were going to call me so soon"?

These kinds of things won't happen if you say *specifically* when you need a reply and when you are going to call. "When" is just as important as "what" if you want to write memos that get people to act promptly and effectively. You don't have to be pushy, just direct: *what* you want done and *when* you want it done by.

How to Write an Effective Memo

Cluster. See pages 14–26.

Freewrite. See pages 27–39.

Rewrite. See pages 40–57.

Write the Subject Line Last. Almost every memo has a subject line. This is the one time we have our reader's complete and undivided attention. *Everybody* reads the subject line. Then, depending on the level of interest, they either read the memo carefully, read it half-heartedly, or throw it away unread.

For writers who want their memos read, the subject line is crucial. It's also the most overlooked part of any memo. Instead of relying on the traditionally lifeless subject lines that characterize most memos—"Copy Machine Use," "Tardiness," "Company Picnic"—try to come up with some real attention grabbers. The subject of the memo and the people who will read it are the best sources for coming up with more creative ideas, but you may wish to generate interest in the form of a question, a line that gets right to the point, or one that announces results or benefits. You may even consider a subject line that has absolutely nothing to do with the memo's subject. Imagine picking up a memo announcing a day off later in the month. That would get your attention. You'd read on. You'd learn that no one is supposed to be using office equipment for personal reasons. "What about the day off?" you'd ask. Then you'd read through the memo again to see where you'd missed what the writer had to say about the holiday.

There are all kinds of tricks we can play on our readers' expectations, but we have to be careful not to abuse this technique. We don't want to wind up like the boy who cried, "Wolf!" Nevertheless, if sometimes our subject lines are straight, at other times, ironic; if the language is sometimes inflated, and sometimes understated and sometimes a parody of subject line language; if our subject lines mimic, taunt, cajole, endear, and inspire, our readers will look forward to and read with increased attention whatever we send them.

Check the Ending. We've given a lot of attention to our opening sentences and subject lines, but our closings should be strong too. This, after all, is where we may present our second most important piece of information or where we tell our readers what we want them to do. It's also our final impression. We want it to be good and we want it to last.

Here are some things to consider:

1. *Don't wrap everything up in a summary paragraph.* The reader has heard it all before and will resent having to sit through it again. Instead, pick out one point or one specific action and repeat that in such a way as not to sound as if you're repeating it. "I look forward to hearing your reaction to . . ." and "I look forward to seeing how you handle . . ." are two ways of restating points.

2. *Save something for a handwritten postscript.* Studies have shown that people often read a handwritten postscript first, read it again when they finish the main body of a memo or letter, and remember it longer than anything else. Now this doesn't mean that we should put crucial information in our postscripts. Our readers would wonder why we didn't tell them sooner or how we could have forgotten something so critical. Nor does this mean we should end every memo or letter with a handwritten postscript. What it does mean is that strong closings and handwritten postscripts affect our readers. Nevertheless, we have to be careful. We don't want to push our readers too far or too often. A minor but still important point or some personal note is not only appropriate, it works.

Cheryl Reimold offers two other suggestions for effective closings:

1. Show goodwill—that's what the reader will leave with.

2. Remind readers in tactful terms what they should *know* from reading your memos or what they should *do* after having read them. Do this without making it seem as if you're repeating yourself.

Questions to Ask to Make Sure You've Written an Effective Memo

Is It Personal? Have I used pronouns like "you," "I," and "we" instead of "one"? Have I written as closely as possible to the way I speak? Have I used contractions like "can't," "won't," "I'm," and "they're" to maintain the illusion of a personal speaking voice?

Are My Ideas Arranged Effectively? In some cases, a chronological order is called for; in others, a step-by-step process. Sometimes, if you're trying to persuade someone to share your point of view, you may want to argue from the general to the specific or from the causes to the effects. If you wish to make a comparison that will allow your reader to consider all the facts before making a decision, you can list all the reasons that favor a certain action, followed by all the reasons which don't. If you favor a certain action but wish to come across as impartial, simply list the arguments against your side first, then make sure all these arguments are responded to, before presenting arguments favorable to your position. Or you may wish to divide your subject into several parts, listing the pros and cons within each part. This is the most sophisticated way of comparing and contrasting two viewpoints, because both sides of every argument are stated together. The reader can read, think, and respond to both at once. To influence the reader's perspective, once again state the position you favor as a response to something you've already presented.

Compare some overly obvious descriptions of politicians running for office in Michigan. A local newspaper that had endorsed one of the candidates wrote that, after giving a speech, the crowd-pleasing candidate jumped into a sedan and took off for the airport. The other candidate, meanwhile, was seen slouched in the back seat of a waiting limousine. "Jumped" vs. "slouched," "into" vs. "in the back seat," "sedan" vs. "waiting limousine" all create positive images for the endorsed candidate and negative ones for the other.

When it comes to structuring memos, however, few arrangements are more reliable than or as easy to create as the one that puts the most important idea first, second most important idea last, and everything else in between (see page 12). Even some chronological events may be presented this way. Who says, for example, that the minutes of a meeting have to be presented in the order they occurred? Why can't the most interesting or exciting information— the information our readers are most interested in—be mentioned first?

For those writers who feel more comfortable placing their hard-wrought ideas in a proven formula, Sherry Sweetnam's *The Executive Memo* suggests this four-paragraph structure:

Purpose

Problem

Solution

Follow-up

Almost any message can be written into this effective formula. Simply state the purpose of your memo in the first paragraph, the specific problem you wish to focus the reader's attention on in the second paragraph, the solution to the problem in the third, and what action you want taken in the fourth.

The problem with formulas, however, is that they aren't organic. They encourage us to impose a structure on our subject instead of letting our subjects reveal their own more naturally effective arrangements.

Take this memo, for example:

RE: TARDINESS

It has recently been brought to our attention that many employees are continually arriving at work after the designated arrival time.

This is not pursuant to company policy.

All employees are hereby notified that they must observe the arrival times that have been determined for them.

Please re-implement this policy.

The message that people are late and should come to work on time could be stated in several more effective ways.

The writer could appeal to the latecomers' sense of fairness to the other employees; the writer could inform the latecomers what they cost the company in terms of production, profit, and personal income; the writer could threaten the tardy ones with some reduction in pay or having to make up for lost time after everyone else has gone home. Other reasons would come to mind if we knew the writer's particular situation. Because this writer believed Sweetnam's formula held the key to effective memos, however, he tried harder to meet its requirements than to create a message that worked. Notice how hard the writer strained to get a purpose paragraph, a problem paragraph, a solution paragraph, and an action paragraph. The writer tried so hard, in fact, that he didn't get much else. The memo lacks substance as well as bite and reveals, almost more than anything else, the writer's condescending, authoritative attitude toward the reader. In short, by relying too heavily on a formula and not bothering or caring to question how his readers might react, the writer created a memo that would make most people want to show up late for work to spite him.

Would Any Headings, Lists, Tables, or Graphs Help Clarify My Meaning? Concrete language and personal details are two ways of being specific, but nothing helps the images these words create in our minds as much as a heading, list, table, or graph. Each draws the reader's eyes into our message and delivers our information in a succinct, powerful way.

The headings that punctuate this book offer good examples of what we're talking about. Open to any page that has one. Notice how your eyes are naturally drawn to the heading? You almost *want* to read that first. You do, in fact, read that first. And the bolder the heading (italics, capital letters, colored letters, amount of white space around the heading), the stronger the draw.

Headings

The United States Customs Service came up with a creative heading to stand out from the other headings in its booklet, *Know Before You Go*, for Americans traveling overseas (Figure 9). But even something as eye-catching as that handsomely wrapped package can be overdone. Collecting all the headings of all the subjects in the booklet, the Custom's editors created a monster. Our eyes are bombarded with so much stimuli, the messages are lost (Figure 10). In the trade, this kind of approach is called "visual indigestion."

Lists

Lists pick up where headings leave off. They reduce complex information into parts our eyes and minds can handle one at a time. Compare two announcements from our friends at the Internal Revenue Service (Figure 11). Do you notice how, looking at the example on the left, you don't want to read it? Somehow you just know it says something you don't want to hear? Compare that with the result of the government's decision to make our IRS forms readable. Notice how your eyes are drawn to the image the list makes on the page? They begin to ferret out meaning around the numbers and white space almost before you're aware of what you're doing.

And what about the language! We may not like the message we read but, in the improved version, at least we understand that we're being threatened. Most readers of the original sentence would give up before the threat had been made.

Tables and Graphs

Tables and graphs, like headings and lists, enable us to highlight selected material. Imagine having to rely only on

RESIDENCY

RETURNING RESIDENT. If you leave the United States for purposes of traveling, working, or studying abroad, and return to resume residency in the United States, you are considered *returning U.S. residents* by Customs.

Residents of American Samoa, Guam, or the U.S. Virgin Islands who are American citizens are also considered returning U.S. residents.

LIQUOR, TOBACCO, AND PERFUME containing alcohol worth over $5 retail are excluded from the gift provision. Persons cannot send "gifts" to themselves or to others traveling with them. Gifts ordered by mail from the U.S. do not qualify under this duty-free gift provision.

GIFTS YOU BRING WITH YOU, whether given to you by others or intended for someone else, may be included in your $400 or $25 exemption. You may not include gifts for business, promotional, or other commercial purposes.

GIFTS YOU SHIP FROM ABROAD, if worth $50 or less in fair retail value where shipped, can be received in the U.S. free of duty and tax if the same person does not receive more than $50 in gift shipments in one day.

Figure 9

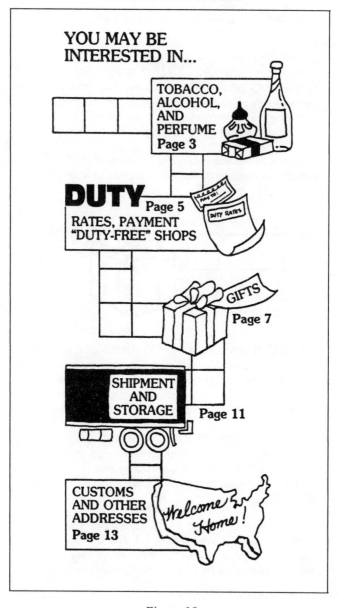

Figure 10

1976	1977
The Privacy Act of 1974 provides that each Federal Agency inform individuals, whom it asks to supply information, of the authority for the solicitation of the information and whether disclosure of such information is mandatory or voluntary; the principal purpose or purposes for which the information is to be used; the routine uses which may be made of the information; and the effects on the individual of not providing the requested information. This notification applies to the U.S. Individual	The Privacy Act of 1974 says that each Federal Agency that asks you for information must tell you the following: 1. Its legal right to ask for the information and whether the law says you must give it. 2. What purpose the agency has in asking for it, and the use to which it will be put. 3. What could happen if you do not give it.

Figure 11

prose to convey information provided in the table and graph presented in Figures 12A and 12B.

The Final Presentation: How to Make It Look Good

Now that you've thought of everything that should be included in your memo, freewritten these ideas to give your reader the impression of natural speech, rewritten your prose to make your meaning as clear as possible, and de-

CONVERTING TO METRIC

Many countries have converted to the metric system of measurement. It's not difficult—just different. Here are some hints for handling kilometers (km), liters (L), and degrees Celsius (°C).

Taking the worry out of being close

Distances and speed limits are posted in kilometers. A kilometer is about 0.6 of a mile, and a mile is 1.6 km. To find the approximate mile equivalent, drop the unit or right-hand digit of the km number and multiply by 6. For instance:

100 km/hour = 10 × 6 = 60 miles/hour
90 km to Medicine Hat = 9 × 6 = 54 miles

Kilometer Speedometer

Miles	30	40	50	60			
Km	40	50	60	70	80	90	100

Shopping—How much bang for your buck?

Yard goods are now sold by the meter (m), groceries and packaged goods by grams (g) or kilograms (kg), and liquids by liters (L).

Length

1 inch	= 2.5 cm	1 cm = 4 inches
1 foot	= 30 cm or 0.3 m	
1 yard	= 90 cm or 0.9 m	1 m = 3.3 ft
1 mile	= 1.6 km or 1600 m	1 km = 6 mile

Figure 12A

TEMPERATURE CONVERSION

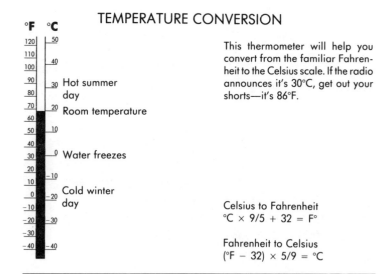

This thermometer will help you convert from the familiar Fahrenheit to the Celsius scale. If the radio announces it's 30°C, get out your shorts—it's 86°F.

Hot summer day

Room temperature

Water freezes

Cold winter day

Celsius to Fahrenheit
°C × 9/5 + 32 = F°

Fahrenheit to Celsius
(°F − 32) × 5/9 = °C

cided whether your memo can be made more effective through visual aids, you're ready for the final presentation.

Because your reader will see your memo before reading it, you want to make it look good. Here are some suggestions for a successful first impression.

Don't Squeeze as Much as You Can into a Small Space. Remember those examples from the Internal Revenue Service? Let them be your guide. Leave plenty of white space around what's important to the reader: his or her name (spelled correctly), the date, whom the memo is from, and the subject line. At least four line spaces should separate this information from the main body of the message, and two line spaces between each paragraph will also help your memo's appearance.

Keep the Opening Paragraph Short. We don't want to overwhelm our readers but ease them into the main body of our memo. Using short sentences and a short opening paragraph helps us do this. As a rule of thumb, the more important or complicated the information, the shorter the opening sentences and paragraphs should be.

Vary the Length of the Remaining Paragraphs. Many writing consultants recommend that no paragraph be more than five or seven lines long and that no sentence contain more than seventeen words. Although there is some truth to shorter sentences and paragraphs being easier to understand than longer sentences and paragraphs, the deeper truth is that excessive uniformity kills. To put a limit on anything is to put an unnecessary limit on ourselves. Let the subject determine its length. Something that looks good but whose breaks are found to be forced and inappropriate reflects just as badly on the writer as writing with no breaks whatsoever. Both show an insensitivity to language and to our readers.

Be Consistent. If you indent the first paragraph, indent the rest. If you begin in the present tense, stay in the present tense unless you have a good reason to switch to the past or future. And when you make your switch, announce it beforehand by beginning a new paragraph.

Be Correct. The names of the people you write to are most important. Then all other words. Misspelled words, as well as certain grammatical constructions, create what some writers call the "Teeth and Spinach" effect. Have you ever gone to lunch with someone who's had some food caught on their teeth? Your companion is talking, but all you pay attention to is the food? Certain kinds of errors, of which misspelled words may be the most damaging, invite the same kind of reaction: They stand out more than the message.

Keep It Clean. Make sure your memo leaves without wearing what you had for lunch. This is an extension of the "Teeth and Spinach" syndrome. Try to remove any fingerprints, smudges, stains, or eraser marks that may give the impression you're careless.

Sign Your Name So People Can Read It. We sign our names rather than type them in because we want to be personal. In many memos, they are the only sign of life. So make the most of it: large enough to show we have confidence in ourselves, legible so our readers know we care about them.

If You Don't Make It Look Good, Make It Look Interesting. One of the best memos I've received came from Tom Joseph, a vice-president at National Seminars, Inc. It stood out so much from the others I received that day that I read it first. Later I found myself telling others about it. It's short, to the point, humorous, gently recommends I push the

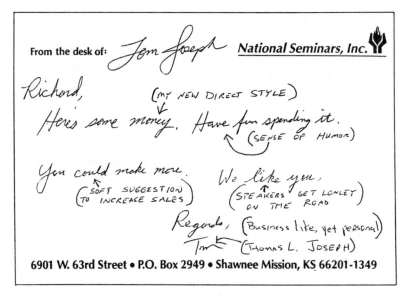

Figure 13

company's products harder, and successfully parodies some points Tom heard me make in a speech on the increasing dehumanization of our prose styles. His memo, more than anything else, reeks of humanity (Figure 13). Another of my favorite memos comes from Gryphon House, Inc. (Figure 14). And how about this parody of legal writing?

RE: MANUAL COMMUNICATORS

Know all men by these present that I hereby give, grant, bargain, sell, release, convey, transfer, and quit claim all my right, title, interest, benefit, and use whatever in, of, and concerning this chattel, otherwise known as MANUAL COMMUNICATORS, together with all the appurtenances thereto of wood, lead, paint, metal, and erasers to have and to hold said pencils together with its box of cardboard to yourself and your heirs in fee simple forever, free from all liens, encumbrances, easements, limitations, restraints, or conditions whatsoever, now or anywhere made to the contrary notwithstanding with full power to scribe, chew, erase, or otherwise utilize said COMMUNICATORS, or give away with or without full erasers or sharpened points.

These memos work because each one, in its own way and for different reasons, stands out from all the other memos we read. Which is exactly what the people who wrote them intended. They know that the problem with most memos is not that their writers are all trying to be the next Tom Wolfe but that they are all trying to sound like stalwarts in the gray flannel suit brigade.

If you want to sound like one of that crowd, a dull,

Here at Gryphon House, we get a big kick out of screaming at our book-packer persons. The only problem is we were running out of excuses. Then we came up with this idea: We asked our packers to sign this slip and place it in the box with your order.

So, if the packer messed up your shipment, *please* let us know. Contact us at:

GRYPHON HOUSE INC.
Screaming Mad Dept.
3706 Otis Street P.O. Box 275
Mt. Rainier, Md. 20712
or call
(301) 779-6200

This order was packed by _____ X _____

Packer's Signature

Figure 14

tedious, unimaginative vocabulary is your ticket. If, on the other hand, you wish to rise above the masses, interesting creative memos are one sure way to do it. Why? Because yours will be the ones people will read, listen to, and respond to. You'll be the one whose memos make a difference. You'll be the one everyone looks forward to hearing from. You'll be the one who's answered the call for simple, clear, understandable prose.

LETTERS

> In general those who have nothing to say contrive to spend the longest time doing it.
> —*James Russell Lowell*

A business letter, like any other piece of writing, delivers its message on two levels. The first is the literal message itself; the second is the kind of relationship the message establishes between the writer and the reader. In other words, *what* is said and *how* it is said are so intertwined they are inseparable. Every writer must weigh both regardless of the subject. How well the writer has managed to communicate on each of these combined levels can be measured by the reader's response.

To get the response we want from our readers, we have to know two things before we begin any letter: our subjects and our audience. In fact, nothing will sabotage our letters faster or more thoroughly than a display of ignorance on either count.

Our Subjects

How well do you have to know your subject before you can begin writing about it? The answer of the sages: Well enough to explain it to someone not in the field.

We show our readers how well we know our subjects by focusing their attention on the information most important to them. The ability to separate the vital from the superfluous will carry us in much better standing with our readers than any big words or convoluted sentence structure. In fact, the first sign of writers who don't know what they're talking about is the language they use to mask their ignorance or insecurity.

Our Readers

The words we use to describe our subjects reveal more than how much we know about them, however. They also establish our attitude toward our readers. Tone of voice—conversational, distanced, apologetic, authoritative, whatever—indicates whether the letter is to a subordinate, an equal, or a superior. This doesn't mean that all letters to all bosses should be obsequious or that all letters to all subordinates should be condescending. What it means is that, as writers, we have to be aware of how our readers perceive us through the messages we send them. This relationship with our readers is built or damaged by the tone of voice that conveys the information we send. In many ways, tone is more important than information. Unfortunately, tone is also difficult for writers to read in their own letters. What we may think is strong, others may see as inflexible; what we might read as considerate, others might interpret as weak. The important thing is to be aware of this component, to ask ourselves how our readers will take what we say. If there's one impression we should want most of our readers to have, however, it is that we are on their side, that we have their interests at heart.

The more you know your readers, the better the chances of being on their side. When proofreading your letters, try to put yourself in the reader's place. What's in this for the reader? Why should the reader agree with me? What's the reader's perception of our relationship? How will that perception affect the action the reader will take? Can I do anything to improve this relationship?

Some good suggestions for answering this last question appear on pages 164 and 165 of the section on memos. In fact, because business letters are often extended memos, most of what is found in the section on memos also applies to letters. The same is true for prewriting, freewriting, and rewriting. These are the first steps to any kind of writing.

Having prewritten, freewritten, and rewritten our business letter, then, the next step is to place our message in the kind of format our readers expect to see when they pick up any business letter.

The most effective formats, like the most effective letters, are short, clear, and simple. Try to keep your business letter to one page. Busy people don't have time to read long, complex letters. They want their information in clear, concise terms, terms that are as easy to read as possible. The less work we make for them, the more they appreciate us.

Most business letters consist of a date, name and address, subject line, salutation, body, closing, and signature.

Let's take 'em one at a time.

The Date. The traditional way to date a letter is to spell out the month—no abbreviations or numbers only—followed by the day and year: August 21, 1987. The current fashion, however, is a day-month-year sequence with no commas: 21 August 1987. The problem with this construction comes when we adopt its numerical equivalent: 21/8/87 is clear enough, but most Americans would be confused anytime the first two numbers were 12 or less, 12/7/87, for example, or 3/8/88.

Fortunately, most of us have no trouble with either August 21, 1987 or 21 August 1987. Whichever sequence you choose, be consistent. Use it in all your correspondence.

The date is the first line of any business letter. Place it

1½ inches from the top of the page or several spaces below your letterhead. The trend these days is to have the date and everything else "flush left," where it can all be taken in at a glance. Some people, however, prefer the traditional method of placing the date in the upper right hand corner of the page. Both are acceptable (Figure 15).

Name and Address. The address begins with the name of the person we are writing to and it is presented formally: "Margaret Bisset," for example, or "M. L. Carr." The use of titles like "Mr.," "Ms.," "Mrs.," or "Miss" are considered optional at this point in the letter, but it is common to write "Ph.D." or "M.D." after the names of people who have these degrees. "USN," "USMC," and the like are acceptable for people in the military, as are "S.J.," "O.F.M.," or "C.F.X." for clergy. Note that there is no space between the letters in any of these titles, and a comma separates the title from the name: "Margaret Bisset, Ph.D." (Figure 16).

Some people are secure in their accomplishments and don't need to be reminded of them. Others, however, would be offended if you didn't pay homage to their laurels. Feel free to omit the title for healthier egos, especially if you become more familiar with each other and your correspondence increases.

21 August 1987

Figure 15

21 August 1987

Margaret Bissett, Ph.D.

Figure 16

Place the name of the reader's department, if you know it, under his or her name (Figure 17). If you don't know it or there isn't one, write the organization's name, abbreviating only such words as Company (Co.), Incorporated (Inc.), and Limited (Ltd.).

The street or the box number, which appears directly under the organization's name is usually spelled out, though abbreviated versions of Street (St.) and Avenue (Ave.) are not uncommon.

The city, state, and ZIP code make up the final line of the address: "New York, NY 10012" (Figure 18). For the

21 August 1987

Margaret Bissett, Ph.D.
English Department
New York University

Figure 17

21 August 1987

Margaret Bissett, Ph.D.
English Department
New York University
19 University Place
New York, NY 10012

Figure 18

largest cities, it has become popular to omit the state: "New York 10012," "Los Angeles 90045." A place like Columbus, OH, however, should always appear as "Columbus, OH 43215."

Whether you write "N.Y." or "NY" for New York is arbitrary. What is important is getting the abbreviation right. Don't write "MI" for Minnesota (MN) or Mississippi (MS), and don't use "MA" if you mean Maine (ME). If the ZIP code is incorrect, your letter will be returned.

The Subject Line. The subject line, the norm in memos, is gaining acceptance in business letters. Preceded by "RE:" or "SUBJECT:", this line calls our reader's attention to the letter's purpose (Figure 19). It arouses expectations in their minds before they begin to read a word of our message. The subject line can also emphasize what we think is most important.

The Salutation. The salutation (Figure 20) has undergone something of a revolution in the past few years, and the dust still hasn't settled. One thing has become clear, however: "Dear Sirs" and "Dear Gentlemen" are gone and will never return.

21 August 1987

Margaret Bissett, Ph.D.
English Department
New York University
19 University Place
New York, NY 10012

RE: Nominations for the Henry James
    Scholarship

Figure 19

Most salutations begin with "Dear" followed by "Mr." or "Ms." and the reader's name. Except in those few isolated communities where women are still referred to as "girls" or "gals," "Miss" has gone the way of "Sirs" and "Gentlemen." And "Mrs.," unless the woman we're writing to has

21 August 1987

Margaret Bissett, Ph.D.
English Department
New York University
19 University Place
New York, NY 10012

RE: Nominations for the Henry James
    Scholarship

    Dear Prof. Bissett:

Figure 20

indicated she prefers to be addressed by that title, is not very far behind "Miss."

If the reader is a professor, doctor, minister, or member of the military, courtesy demands we address them by their titles: "Dear Prof. Bissett:"; "Dear Dr. Jay:"; "Dear Rev. Ritchie:"; "Dear Capt. L'Heureux:". Note that the use of abbreviations for titles is acceptable—most stylebooks insist on it—and a colon follows each name.

Now for the fun. What do you do if you don't know the reader's name, don't know if the reader is a woman or a man, or don't know if you should call the person by his or her first name?

When you don't know your reader's identity, you can use the salutation "Dear Sir or Madam," but most businesses encourage a preliminary phone call to find a reader's name. These companies have found that letters addressed to specific people are answered sooner and better than those sent to whoever happens to open the mail. This technique is especially effective when the writer spells the reader's name correctly.

As an alternative to this approach, address your letter to the position your reader holds: "Dear Custodian," "Dear Public Relations Officer," or "Dear Customer." Some people see this approach as dehumanizing to the reader, making him or her only a cog in a big machine, and prefer the "Dear Sir or Madam" salutation.

If you're writing to M. L. Carr or I. W. Thomas, don't assume they are men by the positions they hold. Many women use initials because they don't want to be stereotyped; many men use initials because before 1959 it was a popular way to have your ego stroked. Others just enjoy confusing people.

There are three ways to get around this problem:

1. Address the position: "Dear Mr. President."

2. Forget about the title: "Dear M. L. Carr."

3. Drop the salutation altogether. This is something of a fad on the East and West coasts. It saves time, space, and the possibilities for error. Since the reader's name only appears under the date, it may be considered redundant. Advocates of this format also point out that the people we write to in business aren't usually "dear" to us. For this reason, the salutation dropouts also omit closings like "Sincerely" and "Yours truly." They hold, moreover, that no one pays any attention to closings, so the line has become superfluous.

Opponents to this practice claim that this is only one more step in the dehumanization that seems to be sweeping professional communities. Pretty soon we won't be people any more but machines responding by rote to whatever stimuli Big Brother directs at us. Those who no longer hold the salutation and closing in high regard counter with their claim that writers can still be personal by mentioning the reader's name in the letter.

You decide.

When do you address a reader by his or her first name? Follow your intuition. Most readers would think you were impertinent if you called them by their first names the first time you wrote them a letter. They would like to have some say in the matter or at least participate in some way before you become familiar with them. Once people use your first name, however, it would be impertinent not to respond in kind.

This delicate business of deciding when to address people by their first name stems from the nineteenth-century convention of not referring to co-workers or business associates by their first names. To do so was not to know your place. The convention lives on today, among nonprofessionals. It is not uncommon, for example, to hear doctors in a hospital refer to each other as "Sam" or "Susan," while the kitchen workers go around calling each other "Mrs. Johnson" and "Mr. Munroe." Some won't call

you by your first name even if you ask them to. Not only
don't you know your place, you don't know theirs either!

Not to use the first name of a person whom we've spoken
to informally on the phone or one who's signed a first name
at the end of a letter, however, is indecorous. To remain
unnecessarily in a subordinate role or to maintain a formal
distance can be just as damaging as being informal too
quickly.

There are many ways people have of making themselves
feel important. Insisting on titles and reserving the right
to use first names are two of them. Regardless of how lightly
we ourselves may take these conventions, we have to respect
those that hold on to them.

When you do use a first name, continue the standard
practice in the salutation of following it with a colon: "Dear
Kathryn:" or "Dear Joseph:" for example.

The Body and the Closing. The body of any letter presents your message to the reader. It is usually divided into
three parts (beginning, middle, and end). The closing caps
off your letter.

1. THE BEGINNING. There are as many ways to begin a
letter as there are letters to write. The most effective openings, however, are short, clear, easy-to-read, personal, and
grab the reader's attention. Or at least tell our readers what
the letter is about. We can also begin on some point we
share with our readers—a mutual acquaintance, for example—or we can provide our readers with some background information to prepare them for what follows.

Earlier in this book we discussed the most effective way
to write an opening sentence and showed some opening
sentences that have worked well for other writers (see pages
44–46). Additional effective openings include the following:

A question. A question immediately elicits a response from a reader. Almost without realizing it, the reader is involved. The only problem with questions is that they may be overused, and anything overused can be seen as a sign of laziness. Opening with a question, then, requires the kind of creativity that will separate our questions from all the others.

A statistic. But not just a number. Phrase your information so that it is seen as relevant at least and gripping at best.

A point. Generally speaking, the sooner we get to the point in any letter, the better: "I showed up late for work the other day, and I was still the only person in the office."

An attitude. "What amazed me about the veterans was that there were so many of them," "Our values these days seem to center around God and carpets," and "Real estate is the opium of the eighties" all convey a specific attitude toward a subject.

A quotation. "Jean Genet tells us that 'to achieve harmony in bad taste is the height of elegance' " is one way to open with a quotation. Here's another: " 'When I want to read a good book, I write one.' If what Benjamin Disraeli says is true, then . . . ."

Openings we don't want to see in our letters are the ones we've seen before:

This is to further our telephone conversation of . . .

With regard to your letter of July 12, please be informed . . .

The following is in reference to . . .

It has become evident that . . .

For the purpose of finding your missing . . .

Inasmuch as we haven't heard from you . . .

In view of the information received by . . .

The purpose of this letter is to provide an opportunity whereby you may . . .

The key to writing a good opening is to appeal to your readers' interests and experience. Unless they know you and are interested in you as a person, they want only to know how to make their own work easier or cheaper or more effective. Appeal to these needs first, and your readers will respond in ways that will satisfy yours.

2. THE MIDDLE. Once we've gotten our readers past the opening paragraph, we have to maintain their interest. If our opening paragraph worked well, they'll be patient with us, trusting we'll bring them back to the point that grabbed their attention. We can use our second paragraph to fill in whatever background information is necessary or explain in greater detail any claims or promises we may have made. At the same time, we have to remember there is no such thing as a captive audience. We have to prove our message is a must.

Here are some techniques for keeping our readers' interest:

A. Let your enthusiasm for your subject shine through.

B. Don't try to cover too much. Your messages will be complete if you give your readers what they *need* to know.

C. Try to be conversational. Allow the reader to have some idea of who you are as a person.

D. Put people in your writing. You'll get more mileage out of one story about how your product or service helped someone than you will out of all the adjectives in the world.

E. Make sure everything you write is from the reader's point of view.

3. THE END. How we end our letters depends in large part on how well we know our readers. If we know our readers well enough to make a personal comment or reference, they may be disappointed if we don't write one. On the other hand, no comment should be so personal as to attract the attention of anyone else who may read the letter.

If we don't know our reader well, we're probably better off ending the letter after we've said what we want to say. In any case, we don't need to repeat or summarize anything contained in a one-page letter. We can, however, reinforce a major point or directive by saying it in another way. "I hope to hear from you soon about . . ." and "Why don't you give me a call when you finish . . ." are two ways to end our letters without seeming to be repeating ourselves.

If you've written about what you're going to do for your reader, you may wish to end with when you're going to do it. If, on the other hand, your letter discusses something you want your reader to do for you, end with when you need it done by. And why.

A popular ending these days is to offer any help the reader may need in dealing with whatever information is contained in the letter. In these cases, although it's overused, "If I can be of any further help, please let me know" has a personal tone that is lacking in "If I can be of further assistance to you regarding these matters, please do not hesitate to contact this office." Because of its formal structure—and because we've heard it this way before—the latter sentence lacks warmth and sincerity. We feel the writer is only saying it because he or she has to.

Other endings to consider are:

If you send us _____ today, we'll . . .

I'd really appreciate your . . .

If I don't hear from you by _____, I'll . . .

Please help us by . . .

Won't you help me help you by . . .

Thank you for your time and consideration. I look forward to . . .

4. THE CLOSING. The most popular way to close letters in the nineteenth century was to write something like:

With best wishes for continued success, I remain,

Very sincerely yours,

There are still people who favor this kind of closing. Those who don't, call it a bustle and prefer the more simple "Sincerely," because it avoids any suggestion of talking either up or down to the reader.

Other popular closings include:

Cordially,   With best wishes,
Respectfully,   With continued good . . .
Sincerely yours,   With kind regards,
Truly yours,   Yours sincerely,
With best regards,   Yours truly,

"Cheers" and "All the best" have never really caught on. "Protecting the peace," "Yours in the bond," "Sincerely yours in Christ," and "With peace and concern" are reserved for, respectively, the military, fraternities and sororities, the clergy, and former hippies making their fortune in the health food market.

Because most readers are more interested in what we have to say than in how we close our letters, the latest fashion, as mentioned earlier, is to send the closing the way of the introduction: Out.

The Signature. Three important considerations: Write your name in letters big enough to show you are somebody, write it legibly, and leave enough room at the bottom of the page so that your signature doesn't seem cramped or forced in merely as a formality.

If you need a second sheet of paper to make your signature "look right," use one. Your signature is your personal mark. In fact, it is the most personal part of your letter. So give yourself some room to enjoy writing it out. But try not to have just your signature on that second page. The last sentence of your final paragraph is enough to go with it, but the entire last paragraph is better. Whatever you do, try not to break the final sentence of your letter or any word in that sentence between two pages. Like the cramped or forced signature, it gives the impression that your letter hasn't been carefully planned.

Under your signature, of course, comes a printed version of your name, and under that any title you may wish to include (Figure 21). If you prefer to be addressed in a particular way, this may be a good place to let your reader know.

Shirley Levine
Assistant Professor of Humanities

Figure 21

Our final letter, from Professor Levine to Professor Bissett, then, could look something like Figure 22. Professor Levine doesn't include a postscript because to write one in this kind of letter might give the impression that her recommendation wasn't carefully thought out. In less formal letters, however, a postscript can be a useful way to include

21 August 1987

Margaret Bissett, Ph.D.
English Department
New York University
19 University Place
New York, NY 10012

RE: Nominations for the Henry James Scholarship

Dear Prof. Bissett:

I have known Jean Monroe since she was a student in my Victorian Literature class at the University of Michigan in 1984. During that year, Jean impressively demonstrated her genuine love of literature, her perceptive insight into literary techniques and artistic vision, and her ability to express herself both aloud and on paper. It was during the course of two difficult seminars in 1985, however, that I came to admire Jean's alert and inquisitive intellect. Never satisfied with facile solutions or favoring pet interpretations, she is a tireless researcher who mines her material exhaustively and develops insightful interpretations.

Contrary to what the above paragraph might imply, Jean is not your brooding scholarly type, but an attractive, vivacious woman who raises a family and works as everything from a postmistress to a school teacher. How she was able to do these things and lead the best discussion in each of the two seminars—one on *Beowulf* and the other on the films of Max Ophuls—I'll never know, but both classes were examples of the way to turn critical studies into inventive and demanding lessons.

On a personal level, while capable of persuasively defending her own ideas, Jean is always open to suggestions. She is warm, friendly, and gentle, as well as firm, clear-headed, and mature. On the grounds of her intelligence, temperament, command of her material, and articulateness, I judge that she would make a significant contribution in your program and prove herself the kind of graduate student of which New York University can be proud. In short, I recommend her highly and without qualification as a scholar, a teacher, and a human being.

Sincerely,

Shirley Levine

Shirley Levine
Assistant Professor of Humanities
University of Michigan
Ann Arbor, MI 48106

Figure 22

information that wasn't presented earlier, or it can be used to spur the reader to act, as in Figure 23:

P.S. If you can have your report on my desk by Monday, I can . . .

P.S. If you send me your order today, you'll receive . . .

P. S. Postscripts written in your own hand receive more attention, are remembered longer, and are acted on sooner and more effectively than typed or printed postscripts.

Figure 23

PERSUASIVE LETTERS

A clear statement is the strongest argument.
—*English proverb*

We are all expert persuaders. We started when we were infants crying for our parents to pick us up, and we continue to develop and refine our techniques almost every time we open our mouths or pick up our pens. In short, we've been in the business of buying and selling long before we knew what a product was. For most of our lives, we've been selling ourselves—how we look, our ability to think, the techniques we have for articulating our thoughts—and we've been asking others to buy our products—ideas, services, directives, even works of art.

To increase people's knowledge, to get them to agree with us, to change the way they do something, to inspire them to act, we have to know what they know: what they value, what they're biased against, why they behave the way they do, what motivates them more than anything else.

We also have to know ourselves and what specifically we want our readers to do: learn, agree, act, whatever. Knowing our needs and our goals, we present them in the words and interests of our readers.

To do this successfully, we must continue to use the techniques we've already developed: grabbing the reader's attention in the opening paragraph; keeping our messages short, clear, and simple; writing in our own natural voices; being personal and enthusiastic; arranging our ideas effectively; making our letters look good; and ending them on a note that encourages our readers to act.

There are, however, several other criteria that come into play when we consciously try to persuade someone:

Respect Your Readers. Don't talk down to them. The *New York Times*, *The New Yorker*, and *The Atlantic Monthly* don't print stories that can be read by people who haven't graduated from high school because they think their readers are stupid. The people who run and contribute works to these publications want their material read. They've learned the most effective way to build an audience is to be clear and direct. They know that a big vocabulary doesn't mean big words; it means knowing many words so that the right one can be chosen for any specific situation.

But these publications aren't trying to persuade. They're trying to inform and entertain. To persuade we have to take our respect for our readers one step farther. We have to accept the fact that people can disagree with us for reasons based on neither stupidity nor malice.

To avoid looking down on your readers, or at least keep them from knowing you don't think highly of them, focus primarily on your subject. If you want your readers to agree with you or at least to consider what you have to say, it might be best not to be too personal. Using "you" and "I" in certain volatile issues—abortion, the environment, nuclear energy—can often distract readers. They think they're being criticized and respond by attacking us rather than listening to what we have to say.

Begin Where You Can Agree. If you know your reader will object to your ideas or proposals, try to find some point you can both agree on. If you can't find one, make one up. You might agree, for example, that your letter focuses on something important for the two of you. Or if you expect a lot of resistance, you might mention that no solution is possible if we let ourselves be hampered by preconceived ideas.

Select the Appropriate Tone. Have you ever read a memo or letter in which the opening sentence of every paragraph sounds like "Now hear this:" or "Only an idiot would think . . ."? Tone is crucial in any form of persuasion, and the most appropriate tone is usually calm, courteous, and objective.

Anticipate Objections. Sometimes we think because we've answered all the valid objections our readers might have, we've done our job. The truth is we've only done half of it. Answer the invalid objections as well. Sometimes, because they are often more emotional than rational, the invalid objections are even more important than the valid ones.

Time Your Message. The best time to persuade anyone of anything occurs when these three circumstances are present:

1. The reader recognizes a need for what you have to offer.

2. The reader has no other pressing concerns to keep him or her from focusing full attention on what you have to say.

3. The reader hasn't already decided to accept a competing recommendation. If the reader has, wait until the competing solution fails before submitting yours, or tailor your suggestions to strengthen any weakness in the policy already in place.

The persuasive letter in Figure 24 greets participants attending a seminar on business writing. Each person has paid almost seventy dollars to attend—many expect to be disappointed in their investment. And who knows what may have gone wrong on the way to the seminar? On top of that, writing is a subject many people don't have positive feelings about. In fact, most of the participants are there because their bosses made them go or because they are so insecure about their writing ability they're ready to try anything.

Not a good place to begin, but the writer knows that if he can make the participants comfortable and prepare them to make the most of *their* seminar, he's going to have converts at the end of the day.

SALES LETTERS

Living in an age of advertisement, we are perpetually disillusioned.

—*J. B. Priestley*

All sales letters have one purpose: to sell. Not every sales letter, however, tries to close a deal. Many are intended to open one, to convince people to consider what we have to say. A second step may be to order our catalogue, telephone one of our representatives, come to our store, let us visit them, or receive something on a trial basis.

Dear Seminar Participant,

Welcome to Powerful Business Writing Skills! You have an exciting session ahead.

We hope you will learn new approaches to writing that you can immediately put to work back on the job. However, because today's learning session is very much a joint effort (you will be working as hard as we will!), we offer some suggestions to help you make the most of what you gain from our program:

- Build on the practical examples your leader describes that help bring to life the concepts presented. How? By relating these examples to your own work situation.

- Take meaningful notes as your leader guides you through the workbook. Also, jot down projects, people, goals, and other related ideas that come to mind as you listen. These notes will be helpful later in setting your action plan.

- Review periodically the material you take with you. Use your workbook as a reference in the office.

We are proud to welcome you to this National Seminars' presentation, and we are confident you will regard the investments of your time and money as good ones.

Sincerely,

Jerry Brown
President

Figure 24

Prewriting

Here are some steps to consider for writing a sales letter that gets people to take action that will eventually lead to a sale:

- Cluster what you want readers to do.

- Cluster all the reasons why your reader should do what you say. How does your product, service, or idea benefit your reader?

- Cluster any limited time offers you can make to entice your reader to act soon: discounts, rebates, bonuses, free gifts, combination packages, extended warranties, free consultations, free accessories, willingness to undersell any competitor, whatever. You know best what you best have to offer.

- Choose only the most important ideas in your clusters. Mark them down in a list, turn the list into an outline with the most important idea first, and then freewrite your rough draft.

Writing

Having arranged your thoughts in the order you want to say them and freewritten them out on paper, see if your message can be improved by satisfying these basic criteria:

- Does the opening sentence grab the reader's attention? Is the reader's curiosity aroused? Here are several proven ways to open any business letter:

- Start out strong: "If you think small refrigerators are cheaper than big ones, think again. At Davenport Appliances, we'll show you . . ."

- Begin with a story: "Growing up in Newark, I learned which sneakers were best for climbing chain-link fences. I may not have to climb fences anymore, but I still need sneakers to . . ."

- Open with a reference to someone you both know. "Joey Prendergast of Simon & Schuster tells me you're looking for a book on bicycles."

- Have I stated clearly and thoroughly what will most benefit my reader? It's important here not to exaggerate. When we write, we establish a certain kind of trust with our readers. If we do anything to break that trust by exaggerating our claims or perhaps failing to distinguish between what is fact and what is opinion, we'll never win back that trust, no matter what we do. Be honest. There's no reason to put on airs. People who try to impress others with what isn't real wind up impressing only themselves.

  And think twice about downgrading a competitor. Even if you're honest, you may come off as being unfair.

- Have I made it easy for my reader to respond? Should I include a self-addressed envelope, discount coupon, toll-free number, or free-delivery offer?

Rewriting

Just to make sure what you've written is the best of all possible sales letters, go through the following checklist:

- Do I get the reader's attention?

- Do I maintain it?

- Have I stated the reader's benefits clearly and honestly?

- Is my letter personal?

- Is it positive?

- Are my ideas arranged in the most effective order?

- Have I written as closely as possible to the way I speak?

- Do I seem natural as opposed to forced or contrived?

- Should I underline my most important points? Judicious underlining makes any page livelier and reinforces important points, but might my reader think me condescending?

- Would a handwritten postscript or printed quotation at the top of the letter help my purpose?

- Can I use phrases like "preferred customer" or "our pride in this product" so that the reader knows he or she is special and my company isn't trying to unload something it no longer wants?

- Should I prepare my reader for some follow-up? A phone call, visit, or another letter perhaps?

How does the letter in Figure 25 match up against this checklist? Can it be improved or is it good as it is?

LETTERS OF COMPLAINT

The more we proceed by plan the more effectively we may hit by accident.
                                        —*Friedrich Dürrenmatt*

How to Write a Letter of Complaint

Answer these five questions before writing any letter of complaint:

What Do I Want to Achieve? If you simply want to express your anger and you don't care about the conse-

5 January 1988

Mr. LeRoy Musgraves
Resident Director
Dorland Mountain Arts Colony
P.O. Box 6
Temecula, CA 92306

Dear Mr. Musgraves:

We've discovered that many directors of artist colonies—particularly those in rural areas—spend a lot of time running back and forth to the nearest town for supplies.

Why not let us come to you?

If you fill out the enclosed card, checking off a day and time most convenient to you, we'll send our representative to take your order. Any supplies the representative may not have on hand will be delivered the following day.

To help you with your needs, I've enclosed a copy of our catalogue. If there is something you want that is not listed, our representative will be happy to get it for you.

Enjoy the time you won't spend running to town.

Sincerely,

Donna Hall
Sales Manager

Figure 25

quences, go ahead and write whatever you wish, however you wish to say it. But be warned: letters of complaint that are too aggressive or angry don't wind up in the wastepaper basket; they wind up in the wrong people's files. And like guns in Alfred Hitchcock movies, they come out firing sooner or later.

Who Can Best Help Me? If you want a refund or to correct a mistake and already have a contact in the company, write to that person. If you don't get the results you want or don't know anyone in the first place, write to the president. If you still don't get what you want, write to the Better Business Bureau, your state's consumer affairs bureau, or some other regulatory agency and send a copy of your letter to the president.

How Much Does My Reader Know? Unless you know differently, assume your reader knows nothing. He or she will respect you for presuming their innocence—even if they're guilty—and be more willing to help you.

Also, if you wish to display your anger, this is the place to do it. Get all those horrible feelings off your chest; just don't hold your reader responsible. You need him or her to sympathize with you and help you.

Can I Document This? Send along a copy of any receipts you may have or, in special circumstances, the names of witnesses to any injustices you may have suffered.

Should I Let This Cool? If you were angry when you wrote your letter of complaint, the answer is probably yes. Anger has a way of distorting our perception. So write your letter when you're hot—the hotter you are, the more heated the letter—then put it into a drawer for twenty-four hours. If your anger hasn't misrepresented you or what happened, send it when it comes out.

Let's look at the body of a letter of complaint (Figure 26) to see what we can learn from it.

The shipment of 200 textbooks we ordered on April 1, 1987, for delivery on August 1, 1987, did not arrive.

I telephoned you on August 2, and you said you couldn't believe they hadn't come. You said six weeks was the maximum amount of time you needed, that you usually can deliver in two, and that you'd rush the books I ordered immediately.

It's now September 15 and school has started and the books *still* aren't here. What do you expect the teachers and students to do until you get around to sending them? These students have college entrance exams to take in two months; they need the books to score well on those exams; have you no sense of responsibility?

If you can't have those books here by October 1, cancel my order. I'm not going to waste my time working with you when a dozen other distributors have been courting our business.

Figure 26

Is this an effective letter? It would certainly work better on some people than others, and anyone reading it would try to deliver those books, but some people hold that there's a more effective way, a way to get what we want without making our readers feel diminished or defensive.

The Alternative School for Complaint Letters discourages excessive shows of emotion. If we want our reader's help, we should substitute a complete description of the problem for any ranting or raving. Whining, according to these theorists, also wastes time, energy, and space—ours as well as our readers'. A more effective way to work things out for everybody is to submit an explicit statement on the amends we wish our readers to make, when we want them made, and what we will do if we're not satisfied, as in Figure 27:

You returned my rent check ($550) to my landlady with a notice claiming my account (325-463-99) did not have funds to cover the amount of the check.

Four days before I wrote that check, I deposited $1,000 in your Springfield office. To this day, that deposit has not been credited to my account.

I have given instructions to my landlady to redeposit my check. I expect you to honor it and to write her and me letters of apology for the inconveniences you have caused.

A copy of her letter informing me of the check you refused to pay on and a copy of my deposit slip for September 26 are enclosed.

Figure 27

The Let's Be Friends School suggests a more gentle approach. One that, though firm, recognizes mistakes can happen and seeks to correct a problem that could cost the reader future customers. In other words, as in Figure 28, a letter of complaint that doesn't *sound* like a letter of complaint:

The enclosed piece of wood was found in my cupcake.

I know your quality control department probably works overtime to make sure this kind of thing doesn't happen, but every once in a while it does. Perhaps you may be able to use this splinter to determine where a deficiency in your system may exist.

In any event, I'd appreciate your reimbursing me for the Family Pack of cupcakes I bought. Enclosed is the boxtop, as I threw away the receipt.

Figure 28

How to Answer a Letter of Complaint

If you're at fault:

- Apologize.

- Explain what happened.

- Promise it won't happen again.

- Make amends.

- Say what you're doing to correct the problem.

If you're not at fault:

- Still show some sympathy for the reader.

- Avoid shifting blame back onto the reader. Try to word your letter so that the reader will see he or she is responsible without your actually saying so.

- End on a positive note. And be sincere about it. Most people know a phony when they hear one, and sentences like "We are very grateful to you for your letter of complaint" just don't have a ring of sincerity. People aren't usually grateful to receive a complaint.

The following (Figure 29) is a well-worded reply to the last letter of complaint:

We are upset to hear about the wood found in your cupcake. We have since investigated every step of the baking and packaging process but were unable to discover how it may have gotten into the system. Nevertheless, our quality control inspectors are working hard to make sure it never happens again.

We're relieved to hear you weren't seriously injured, and to compensate for any inconvenience you may have suffered, we are sending you a Family Pack of every product on our line.

If you have any further problems, please contact us.

Figure 29

LETTERS OF REFERENCE

In this world, you must be a bit too kind in order to be kind enough.

—*Pierre Marivaux*

Letters of recommendation, reference, introduction, and nomination can all be handled by following these guidelines:

1. State the reason for your writing in the opening paragraph.

2. Name the person you're introducing, recommending, or nominating and how long you've known him or her. In a letter of introduction, explain the reason for the introduction, what it means for the person being introduced.

3. Be as positive as you can without sounding ebullient. Hemingway tells us a person has a right to be judged by his good moments. Concentrate on these and reinforce them with specific examples.

4. Avoid saying something negative. If your doubts are very strong, however, you might define the limits of your recommendation. This will signal your reservation without your having to come off as a villain.

I have read with interest your description of the center for young writers and artists at Vence. In recommending my friend and former student, Mary Ellen Philips, I am certain that she would benefit richly from the experience of living and working in France. She would also, I know, be a welcome member of the community.

As a student of mine a few years ago, Mary Ellen wrote a sequence of poems that were original, exciting, and finely crafted. She is not only a gifted poet, but a very strong, talented fiction writer as well. During the past year she has devoted herself to a graduate program in literature and criticism. This focus has ultimate value for her as a writer, as she well knows. But academic discipline, for a creative writer has to be planned so as to enhance and not hinder creative work.

Thus she hopes to spend the time at your foundation.

She is altogether deserving and I recommend her to you with enthusiasm. I hope you will grant her a residency.

Figure 30

Not a bad recommendation, but not the kind Mary Ellen would hope for either. The writer's recommendation is positive, but you can tell by the tone of voice that it is not unqualified. Figure 31 shows one that's a little stronger:

My first introduction to Mary Ellen Philips was through her poems. I was one of three judges for the Academy of American Poets contest in 1980. Mary Ellen was one of a handful of winners that year. She won again the following year with a different set of judges. I particularly admire the directness of her work—rare in writing by young poets. She seems to take risks in her poems both in content and in formal experimentation, and I found myself reading with pleasure and occasional astonishment before I remembered to judge.

Later, in the spring of 1982, Mary Ellen was my student in an advanced course in contemporary American poetry. Her contributions to that class were great, and her papers sound and persuasive. Especially appealing is a quality of intellectual exploration that characterizes Mary

Ellen's class and written work. Simply, I think
that in time Mary Ellen will become widely known
as an outstanding poet, and I can think of no
better place for her to develop her craft than at
your colony in France.

Figure 31

The committee of judges considering Mary Ellen's application to the writers' colony were willing to accept her after
reading this letter of recommendation, but only if their
stronger applicants refused acceptance. This next letter
(Figure 32), however, put Mary Ellen into the first ranks:

I *cannot* begin this letter for Mary Ellen Philips
with the typical rote and monotonous opener—
"Ms. Philips has been a student of mine for
_____ years," fill in the blank. Banality in no way
becomes her, has nothing to do with what she is
or has been—as a student of mine.

In the fifteen years I've taught at U. Mass–
Boston there have been only three students in
my classes whose writing has been so splendid,
so head-turning, so damn incredible. Mary Ellen
is one of them.

As a writer, she excels in three areas: expository prose, poetry, and creative writing. What
more could anyone ask for? For one of my
American Lit survey courses she wrote an as-
tonishing paper on the Byzantine social structure in Edith Wharton's *Age of Innocence*. The
best paper in the class.

For the past two years, she won the poetry award of the Academy of American Poets.

For the last course she took from me, one in Adolescence in Literature, she wrote what amounted to a fifty-page novella about a woman whose family teeters on the brink of spiritual wreckage and self-destruction, a teenager whose inner strength meets its match only in the figures of her Yankee grandfather and her boyfriend in Vietnam. Then the young woman loses both of them. At the end of this searing, haunting, lovely narrative comes a moment that is just spellbinding—when the woman returns to reclaim, in part, her grandfather's farm. An uprooted person finally becoming rooted. The descriptions of autumnal countryside are lyrical yet hard—avoiding all picture-postcard smarminess. The dialogue—on target, colorful, revealing. I remember how I saved one class that semester to read extracts from student papers, and how I saved the best for last: Mary Ellen's.

I must admit it—it surprised me to realize that she was as adept in creative writing as she was in expository writing. I had pigeonholed her, wrongly. In the American Literature survey classes she was my brightest student, and she wrote the best, most intelligent, most analytical, and most sensitive papers. After ploughing through a desert of papers on the "greatness" of Gatsby, there would be Mary Ellen's oasis at the end.

When I gave my students a chance to develop themselves in papers that were not strictly academic, in a few of my advanced courses, it was once again Mary Ellen whose papers were the most commanding.

I recommended her highly and without qualification for whatever colony, school, job, or any-

> thing else she might consider applying for. Not only will she make a significant contribution in any field she chooses, she will quickly prove herself to be someone of whom any institution would be proud.

Figure 32

Notice the difference in the tones of voice in each of these recommendations. Regardless of what these writers say, we know what attitude each of them holds toward Mary Ellen Philips. But we tend to believe the final writer knows Mary Ellen better. It's the details that give us this confidence. Whereas the other writers use adjectives like "original," "gifted," "sound," and "persuasive" to describe Mary Ellen's accomplishments, the third writer backs up his adjectives with vivid details. We can see his surprise at pigeonholing her incorrectly. We can see the rootless teenager and the Yankee grandfather. We can see her oasis of a paper waiting at the end of a desert of mediocre interpretations of *The Great Gatsby*. In short, Mary Ellen is the kind of person we want.

REJECTION LETTERS

Tact consists in knowing how far to go too far.
—*Jean Cocteau*

There are many reasons to write a letter containing bad news—rejecting a manuscript, turning down a proposal, denying someone a job—but there is only one aim: to say

"No" without losing your reader's willingness to contribute to you or your organization.

There are many formats for writing letters of rejection, but all agree on three major points:

- Begin with something kind.
- State your message clearly.
- End on a positive note.

The most critical component uniting each of these steps is tone. If our tone of voice is too blunt, we will create hostility in our reader; if it is too soft—couching the bad news in excessive praise, for example—the reader may not understand why he or she has been rejected.

Figure 33 shows a letter that some people would consider clear but inconsiderate of the reader's feelings:

> Dear Michael:
>
> We're not going to use your proposal for either the filing system or the data bank.
>
> If, at some future date, we have a project suited for your talents, we will contact you.
>
> Thank you for thinking of us. We hope that you find a position that will make the best use of your time and skills.

Figure 33

What can we learn from this letter? Plenty. It may adhere to the general practice of being short, clear, and to the point, but it unnecessarily diminishes the reader and will create either hostility or complete avoidance forever. Five years from now, when Michael comes up with a brilliant proposal, the writer of this letter will be one of the first to hear about it but one of the last to be offered an opportunity to make use of it.

Here are some things to do and not do when writing a rejection letter:

Do:

1. *Begin with something kind.* There must be something good we can say about Michael's proposals. At least we can acknowledge the effort that went into it or thank him for submitting it.

2. *Prepare the reader for what's coming.* If we're expecting a letter that will contain either an acceptance or a rejection, we know that if the letter doesn't begin "Congratulations" or "Welcome aboard" or "Let me tell you how grateful I am," bad news has arrived. Nevertheless, we appreciate someone who's considerate enough to soften the blow.

3. *Deliver the news clearly but gently.* We don't want to confuse the reader or create false hopes, but we want to retain his or her goodwill.

4. *Give your reasons for your decision.* Let the reader know where he or she stands. Why, for example, was Michael's proposal turned down?

5. *End on a positive note.* Maybe you have some suggestions for improving the proposal. You can't use the proposal, but maybe you know someone who can. The point is, don't shut the door on your reader. You want him or her to think well of you and your organization and come back to you with better proposals in the future.

Do not:

1. *Bury the bad news.* Sometimes in our consideration for others, we hide our bad news behind a welter of detail or

inflated praise. This only confuses the reader and makes us look foolish. How can we not hire somebody, for example, who has more qualifications than the job requires?

2. *Hide behind company policy.* If policy has determined the rejection, don't just state the policy; give the reasons for the policy.

3. *Talk down to the reader.* Michael feels bad enough as it is without having to suffer our being patronizing or condescending.

4. *Repeat the bad news.* That this even has to be said is shocking, but you'd be amazed at the number of times bad news is repeated in letters. These letters sound almost as if they're saying, "Okay, Michael, just in case you didn't get the message the first time, we're going to hit you with it again."

What do you make of the letter shown in Figure 34?

Dear Michael:

Thank you for your detailed and well-written proposals. We enjoyed seeing your work as well as having the opportunity to get to know you.

Unfortunately, what you have proposed doesn't meet our current needs. Our filing system is too unsophisticated and our data base so obsolete, we can't possibly make the best use of your time and skills.

If we do come up with a project more suited to your talents, we'll certainly call on you.

Figure 34

Obviously a big improvement over the first rejection letter, but still a disaster from any organization's point of view. Why? The second paragraph. Just because you care about Michael's feelings, you don't have to degrade yourself or the company you work for.

Here are some formats that some writers use to say "No" with a "Yes" sound:

Four paragraphs:

+ Say something positive.
+ Say something positive.
− Slip in the negative.
+ Say something positive.

Three paragraphs:

K Kiss Say something kind.
K Kick Say what you have to.
K Kiss Say something positive.

Three paragraphs:

B Build a bridge of sympathy to the reader.
M Sandwich your rejection in the middle.
E End with a positive attitude toward the reader so that the reader will end with a positive attitude toward you.

The important thing to note in each of these formulas is not to delay the bad news too long. As Sherry Sweetnam puts it in *The Executive Memo*: "When people kiss, kiss, kiss us and *then* kick us, we get angry. We feel caught off guard, tricked, and manipulated. The secret is to give a *quick* kiss, and then get on with the kick. Be thoughtful of your reader, but also be straightforward."

With all this in mind, give some thought to the memo in Figure 35:

RE: Monthly Sales Meetings

Mary, I received your note about our past few meetings. For the most part, you are right. They are a waste of time and energy, a forum for egos to hear themselves heard.

On the other hand, they're the only time all month and the only times all year when all the sales people can get together and discuss their problems. For some of us, that's also the only time we get to see each other.

And, in spite of a few who feel they have a contribution to make on every issue—maybe they're showing us how much they care—we do get some important things done. At our last meeting, for example, we agreed to establish a collection of materials that would help us improve our writing techniques.

But your letter brings up another point I'd like to respond to. It is the business of the sales manager to set the agenda for every meeting, but it is the responsibility of the sales staff to determine which direction the meeting will go in. It is, after all, *your* meeting. So maybe we could put our heads together over lunch sometime next week and discuss some of the ways the sales people could participate more creatively. Think about it and let me know. I'll welcome any suggestion short of canceling the meetings altogether.

Figure 35

GOODWILL LETTERS

He who says there's no such thing as an honest man,
you may be sure is himself a knave.
—George Berkeley

There is no end to the number of occasions for which we can send goodwill letters: promotions, awards, fellowships, birthdays, anniversaries, new jobs, special achievements, and more. Similarly, there is no end to the benefits that can be reaped from them. While admittedly useful for business reasons, they are also beyond business. They communicate our human joy in another's happiness. And this joy is most effectively communicated when it's handwritten. It doesn't have to be long, just personal, warm, enthusiastic, and sincere:

Congratulations, Joan! I knew you could do it.

It came as no surprise to us to learn about your recent success, Bill, but we were nevertheless thrilled to hear about . . .

I can't tell you how happy it made me to learn of your recent . . .

In many cases, it helps to be consciously specific. Say you're writing to the husband of a woman who just died and you worked with this woman for several years. Instead of repeating the hackneyed "It's for the best" or "I know how you feel," consider telling a story about the time Janet rescued you from what would have been a disastrous meeting with the board, or the time the two of you cooked up a scheme to mislead your top competitor, or the time it snowed and Janet was the only one to . . . . How did Janet cheer you up, calm you down, make herself indispensable, improve the quality of your life? Say specifically. Show how much you'll miss her.

Here's an opportunity for a goodwill letter that few people seize, mostly because they don't see it: a job well done. Most of us tend to notice something when it's done wrong. How about when it's done right? There are some people out there—agents and vendors are two—who only hear from people when those people are angry or want some mistake corrected. Compliment these people for some of the extra trouble they may have gone to in seeing you or for delivering a product that exceeded your expectations. You'll hear from them again.

LETTERS OF APPLICATION

> Make everything as simple as possible, but not simpler.
>
> *—Albert Einstein*

A letter of application, essentially, is a sales letter. You have to sell yourself and your services to an employer who's weighing the services your competitors have to offer.

Here are some suggestions for winning him or her over:

Grab the Reader's Attention. Favorably. The reader should learn immediately why you are writing and what you can do for him or her. Unless you have well-developed narrative talents, don't waste your reader's time with formalities or unnecessary details. Get to the point. If you are applying for a specific job, say so. If the job has been advertised, say where you read about it. If someone in the company told you about the opening, mention the person's name. If you are not applying for an announced opening, explain the kind of work you're looking for.

List Your Strongest Qualifications. Having caught your reader's attention, you want to convince him or her that you are the best person for that position. Stress what you think will interest your reader most. In addition to noting the most pertinent experience in your résumé, be sure to mention knowledge and abilities that will make a favorable impression but, not directly related to the job you're applying for, are not included in your résumé.

Do not begin this or any other paragraph with "Enclosed is a copy of my résumé." It distracts the reader from your letter. Instead, use this statement to end the paragraph that highlights the most important parts of your résumé.

End with a Request for an Interview. This can be done subtly by saying when you will be available or mentioning where you can be reached if your reader would like to get in touch with you. You might propose that you will telephone the reader in several days to learn his or her response to your letter.

Consider these excerpts (Figures 36–38) from job application letters:

> During the recent APA convention in San Francisco, Dr. Margaret Dole, a family counselor in your clinic, told me of a possible opening in the alcoholic abuse program. My extensive background in counseling alcoholics began when . . .

Figure 36

I have read with great interest your advertisement in the *Washington Post* for a comptroller and wish to be considered for the position. My qualifications include . . .

Figure 37

I am looking for a position in an engineering department in which I will be able to use my training in computers. Might there be such a position in your company?

I recently graduated from Ohio State University with a Bachelor of Science degree in Engineering. Through the university's Computer Systems Engineering program, I served as a Program Trainee in several rotating apprentice positions at Computer Systems International in Columbus. Most of my work there, however, was in computer applications, and I'd like to find a job that is more challenging. Details of the kind of work I did at Computer Systems International, as well as the courses I completed at Ohio State, are contained in the enclosed résumé.

Thank you for your time and consideration. I look forward to hearing from you and may be reached at 614–555–3929 between 9 A.M. and 5 P.M.

Figure 38

There's nothing wrong with the last letter of application, but if the writer had found the answers to these questions, she might have discovered a key for making her letter more effective:

- What does this company do?
- Who owns it?
- Is it profit or non-profit?
- Does it have any ties with the government?
- What services does it provide?
- How large is it?
- Are there branches in other places?
- Is it growing or conserving?
- Are the employees generally happy?
- What benefits does the company offer?
- How does their salary compare with others in the field?
- How well, given my background and temperament, will I fit in?
- What are the company's major strengths and weaknesses?
- How will most of my working time be spent?

These are difficult questions. Company employees can provide many of the answers; it wouldn't hurt to contact one —especially before any interview. A copy of an annual report would also help. Some questions may have to wait for the interview, but the more we can learn about an organization, the more ways we'll have of discussing it and our possible relation to it.

The Résumé

Two points:

- List your most recent experience first.

- Put the most important information first. Your experience is usually more important than your education. Therefore, the list of jobs you've held should precede the list of schools you attended. Unless, of course, you have little or no work experience. In this case, you'll want to emphasize your education.

In listing places of work and education, mention the position you currently hold or your highest degree first. Your qualifications, not the prestige of the organization, should be emphasized. That you have been an office manager at the American Broadcasting System is more important than your having worked for ABC. Similarly, your bachelor's degree in engineering is more important than where you got it. Where you worked and where you went to school, to continue the sequence, are probably more important than when you worked there or when you graduated. The same goes for any awards you may have received. List the award first, then the organization that gave it to you.

REPORTS AND PROPOSALS

The best way out is always through.
—Robert Frost

There are many kinds of reports—research, justification, troubleshooting—but most of them have one thing in common: to help someone make a decision. The difference between most reports and a proposal is that whereas a report may offer the pros and cons for people to study before making a decision, a proposal advocates a particular course of action.

The length of a report or proposal depends on the subject being investigated. Perhaps predictably, longer works tend to be more formal than shorter ones, regardless of the subject. Almost all follow a similar format for one good reason: Busy people can compare conflicting reports or competing proposals more easily if they know more or less where the information they're looking for is located. The format offered in this book satisfies the standard for any report or proposal, though you may wish to add certain features depending on your subject, audience, and purpose.

Prewrite

There are three steps to follow before writing any report or proposal. The more thoroughly these steps are completed, the easier will be the writing.

Ask the Right Questions. You want to determine your objective and your audience. The more narrow your focus, the less abstract and difficult your job will be. So interview the person who's authorized the report or proposal (if you're that person, ask yourself the same questions):

- What's the purpose of this report?
- Who's going to read it?
- What needs to be determined?
- Who is involved in the situation?
- What do they think about the problem?
- Where specifically is the trouble located?
- When did the problem start?
- Have any attempts been made to correct it?
- What are the causes of this problem?
- What keeps it from being solved?

Not all of these questions apply to every situation, but asking them helps you narrow your topic. Ironically, the more limited your boundaries, the more details you'll have to write about. To put it another way, it's easier and a lot more interesting to write and read about the role gasoline played in the Battle of the Bulge than it is to absorb a lesson of the same length on the Allied invasion of Europe during World War II.

Learn About Your Subject. There are three main sources for gathering information on any subject. Each has advantages; each has disadvantages. The advantage of using all three is that each serves as a check on the other. By using all three, you will eliminate the disadvantages in each.

1. *The library.* Most of us don't like to go to the library. We've discovered that our frustration levels are low there. Either that or the place puts us to sleep. The reason for this is the way we were taught to work in the library: consult the card or microfilm catalogue; find what you need on the shelves. If it's not there or you can't find the information you need, go to the periodical index. "Card catalogue," "periodical index"—even the names sound discouraging.

The new, more effective way to go to the library is to march straight to the librarian's desk and throw yourself on his or her mercy. Confess that this is your first time in the library. You'll get all the help you need. Librarians, like so many other people, have been given a bad reputation and a stereotype. In reality, they are among the kindest and most generous of people. Give them a chance to help you; they won't let you down.

2. *Questionnaires and interviews.* The advantage of questionnaires is you can get a lot of information in a short period of time; the disadvantage is you can't get anything substantive. For more detailed, thorough information, you have to conduct interviews with people in the department, the president of the company, maybe even an outside authority.

Here are two tips for making every interview a success:

- If you use a pad and pencil or a tape recorder, listen carefully *after* the interview is over and you've put your recording materials away. People sometimes feel nervous about having their words recorded. They think they'll be held responsible for them. When the tape recorder has been turned off or the pad and pencil put away, people often reveal what has been building up inside and they were afraid to say. Listen for it. Most of the time, it will be the best part of your interview.

- Keep quiet. Silence makes people nervous. They feel pressured to fill the void. So after you get your subject's initial response to your question, don't say anything. See if he or she doesn't come forth with some more useful information, the kind that hasn't been programmed from past interviews.

3. *You.* You are an excellent source of information. Especially when writing about the place where you work or a subject you're interested in. And it's okay in a report or proposal to tell a relevant story about something that happened to you. In fact, it's more than okay: It makes good sense. Writing from the first-person point of view is the most seductive technique a writer has for getting the reader to share his or her perspective.

Narratives about you or people you know can also be used to recount an event, make an analogy, or illustrate a point. If you want to engage your reader, there are few more effective ways than telling a story. It gains, holds, and focuses attention on even the most abstract issues in ways expository prose can only approximate.

Notice the effect of these two paragraphs from Amanda Bennett's report on the human model business at trade shows:

—

I have two blisters on each foot. My shoulders are bare and the drafty hall is freezing, yet I'm sweating with anxiety. Once again, I've forgotten my memorized lines. At my side, a man making disgusting kissing sounds is trying to attract my attention.

Welcome to the exciting, glamorous world of auto-show modeling.

Not only is it real, this passage, written in the present tense as well as from the first person viewpoint, puts us right in the middle of the action. What could bring any reader closer to understanding this experience? Not only does it compress useful information into a few lines, it intensifies and predetermines our reader's response to the subject.

Break Your Information Down Into Small Parts You Can Handle One at a Time. Try to reduce the writing of your report to writing a bunch of brief letters. Write each letter individually, and try not to think of the whole report. Watch the letters pile up. You'll be surprised at how quickly and less painfully you'll finish. This is the same technique developed by marathon runners: If you think about finishing, you never will. Focus on one mile at a time. If that's too much for you, break the mile down into parts. One step at a time, if that's what it takes to finish the mile that will take you to the next mile and so on, all the way to the finish line.

To apply this technique to writing, break your subject down into smaller and smaller parts. Keep these parts separate by placing each part in its own file. Then, after you've arranged the files in the order you want to write about them, break each file down even further—to 3×5 cards, with one idea on each card. When you've finished breaking the material down and gotten from files to cards, arrange the cards in the order you want to present the subject. Say, for example, you've broken all your subject material down into six files. Each one of those files can be broken down into any number of cards.

Next, lay the cards where you can see them all at once. Pick the most important card. Mark that "#1." Pick the second most important card or the card that will best lead you into the first card of the second file. Give that card the last number of all the cards. Arrange the cards in between in the order you want to write about their subjects.

Now repeat this process for all the cards in all the files. When all the cards for all the files have been ordered, you're ready to begin writing.

Freewrite

Go back to the first stack of cards from the very first file. Pick up card #1. Freewrite everything you can think of to say about the subject you've written on that card. When you're finished, do the same for card #2. Repeat this process until you've freewritten about all the cards in the file. Then move on to the second file and freewrite through all the cards you've ordered in that file. As you work from file to file, the pages will quickly add up.

When you've finished freewriting about all the topics on all the cards for all the files, go back and read through everything you've written. As you read, compile on a separate piece of paper a list of all your conclusions. Now this is crucial: When you've finished reading your draft of the proposal or report from beginning to end, you'll have a list of all your conclusions about the subject you've investigated. Turn that list into the introduction to your report or proposal.

In other words, writing a report or proposal isn't much different from writing a letter except that the boundaries are larger and material greater. Both can be prewritten and freewritten, and—this is the most important part in terms of saving time and energy—the first part of each can be written last. In the same way that you write the opening sentence to a letter last, so too should you write the introduction to a report or a proposal last. And the most effective way to do that is from the list of conclusions you've drawn up on your first read-through.

Your list of conclusions can also serve as the basis for your report's or proposal's conclusion. Just make sure it is worded differently than the introduction.

Rewrite

As with memos and letters, there are two ways to rewrite: the fast way and the thorough way. But with reports and proposals, each way is one of two steps in a three-step process; they aren't alternatives.

The first step, then, in rewriting your report or proposal is to rewrite it the fast way (see pages 42–47).

The second step is to package your report or proposal in the kind of format your reader expects. Here's a format that will satisfy all but the most idiosyncratic readers.

The Title Page. The title page should include:

- The title, which should give the reader some idea what your report or proposal is about (in a sense, it is your reader's first introduction to your subject, so make it a good one)
- The company's name
- Your name
- The date you submit the proposal

The Table of Contents. A table of contents isn't always necessary, but it can be especially helpful if your report or proposal contains many subsections.

The Summary or Abstract. The summary or abstract is a one-page condensation of your report or proposal. It may be divided in several ways:

- Problem, conclusions, recommendations
- Major issues, minor issues
- Conclusions and recommendations based on gathered information

The Introduction. The introduction should include:

- A statement about the purpose of your report or proposal
- Your view of the problem or situation
- Your conclusions and recommendations

The introduction may also include:

- The limitations of your report
- The methods you used to gather your information
- Any definitions of unfamiliar terms

The Discussion. The discussion is the main body of your report or proposal. It should:

- State your case
- Substantiate your points with specific details
- Allow your reader to see the thought processes that led you to your conclusions and recommendations

The Conclusion. The conclusion to your report or proposal should:

- Discuss the relevance of your findings
- Discuss any patterns and trends in your subject of study, as well as those in your company and other companies.

The Recommendation. Essentially, this section of your report or proposal tells the reader how to put your conclusions into action.

The Bibliography. The bibliography lists the sources used in writing your report.

The Appendix. This section presents any data not included in the main body of your report or proposal that support or expand upon points made in your main body.

The Index. An index is a detailed table of contents. It lists in alphabetical order almost every subject discussed in your report or proposal. In all but the most lengthy and complicated cases, an index is superfluous.

The third step in the rewriting process is to rewrite the now packaged report or proposal according to the guidelines presented in the section on thorough revising (see pages 47–57). In addition to these suggestions, you may also wish to take a second look at how you presented any statistics in your report or proposal. Statistics can easily become the bane of any writer because they have to be included but there's not much you can do with them other than dump them into a graph or table.

Or so it seems. One way of giving life to statistics is to place them in a context. Peter Jacobi tells us that "the straightest approach to the mind is through the heart; the quickest way to the intellect is through the emotions." A narrative as an illustration of statistics does both, but how do you enliven statistics like "The company made a million dollars last year"?

Give them meaning. Place them in a context we can appreciate. That million dollars: Is it up or down from last year? How much? Is that as good or as bad as it seems? Why or why not? And how will the money be spent?

We're all familiar with our national debt. The annual interest on it is over ninety-six billion dollars. It will soon reach a trillion. But what does that mean in terms we as readers can understand and appreciate? How much is ninety-six billion dollars really? It's a lot: more than the combined profits of America's top 500 companies, more than the government spends every year on health, education, and welfare, and more than a stack of thousand dollar bills sixty-seven miles high.

Use your statistics to make a point. Find a way to show your readers just how meaningful they are.

8

*C*ONCLUSION

THE FINAL WORD

> How can I tell you what I think until I see what I've said?
>
> —*E. M. Forster*

There is only one conclusion where writing is concerned: Does it work? If it works, it's right.

The best example of "Does it work?" was told to me by Kathleen Mohn, a speaker for National Career Workshop's Powerful Business Writing Skills program. The story goes that a sales manager in Illinois had one of his representatives in Minnesota quit right in the middle of the selling season. Desperate to find a replacement, the sales manager hired over the phone the first someone who knew someone else who knew someone else who happened to call. Any reference checking would have to wait.

Two weeks after the new man is hired, this letter arrives on the sales manager's desk:

Dere Bos:

I have seen this outfit which ain't never bot a dimes worth of nothing from us and I sole them a cuple hunerd thowsand dolars of guds.

I am now going to Chacawga.

Realizing he's hired an illiterate to represent the company in the northern Midwest, the sales manager begins looking for another representative. Before he can find one, however, this telegram arrives from Chicago:

> I cum hear and sole them haff a millyun.

Now what's he going to do? He's looking to fire someone who should be given a raise. Unable to reach a solution, the sales manager dumps everything into his president's lap.

A weekend goes by. People coming into work on Monday notice that everything that was on the company bulletin board on Friday has been replaced by three pieces of paper: the letter from Minnesota, the telegram from Chicago, and this announcement from the president of the company:

> We been spending to much time trying to spel instead of trying to sel. Let's wach thoes sails. I want everybody shud reed these letters frum Gooch, who is on the rode doin a grate job for us, and you shud go out and do like he done.

BIBLIOGRAPHY

Andersen, Richard. *Powerful Business Writing Skills.* Six cassette tapes and workbook. Overland Park, Kan.: National Seminars Press, 1987.

Bernstein, Theodore. *The Careful Writer.* New York: Atheneum, 1965.

Brown, Leland. *Effective Business Report Writing.* Englewood Cliffs, N.J.: Prentice-Hall, 1963.

Corbett, Edward P.J. *The Little English Handbook.* Glenview, Ill.: Scott, Foresman, 1987.

Dumaine, Deborah. *Writing to the Top: Writing for Corporate Success.* New York: Random House, 1983.

Ewing, David. *Writing for Results in Business, Government, the Sciences, and the Professions.* New York: Wiley, 1979.

Forer, Bruce. *Why We Write.* New York: Harper & Row, 1986.

Hall, Donald. *Writing Well.* Boston: Little, Brown, 1976.

Iles, Robert. *Techniques to Improve Your Writing Skills.* Overland Park, Kan.: National Seminars Press, 1987.

Murray, Donald. *Writing for Your Readers.* Chester, Conn.: The Globe Pequot Press, 1983.

Poe, Roy. *The McGraw-Hill Guide to Effective Business Reports.* New York: McGraw-Hill, 1983.

————. *The McGraw-Hill Handbook of Business Letters.* New York: McGraw-Hill, 1983.

Qubein, Nido. *Communicate Like a Pro.* Englewood Cliffs, N.J.: Prentice-Hall, 1983.

Reimold, Cheryl. *How to Write a Million Dollar Memo.* New York: Dell, 1984.

Ricco, Gabrielle. *Writing the Natural Way.* Los Angeles: Archer, 1983.

Ruggiero, Richard. *The Art of Writing.*

Shurter, Robert L., and Donald J. Leonard. *Effective Letters in Business.* New York: McGraw-Hill, 1984.

Stone, Wilfred. *Prose Style.* New York: McGraw-Hill, 1983.

Strunk, William, Jr., and E. B. White. *The Elements of Style.* New York: Macmillan, 1959.

Sweetnam, Sherry. *The Executive Memo.* New York: Wiley, 1986.

Walpole, Jane. *The Writer's Grammar Guide.* New York: Simon & Schuster, 1984.

Williams, Joseph. *Style: Ten Lessons in Clarity and Grace.* Glenview, Ill.: Scott, Foresman, 1979.

Zinsser, William. *On Writing Well.* New York: Harper & Row, 1976.

INDEX

ABOUT THE AUTHOR

Richard Andersen has been teaching people to write for more than twenty years. A former James Thurber Writer-in-Residence at Ohio State University and Fulbright Professor at the University of Bergen in Norway, his books include three novels, *Muckaluck, On the Run,* and *Straight Cut Ditch,* and two critical studies, *Robert Coover* and *William Goldman.* The author's most recent work, *Arranging Deck Chairs on the Titanic: Crises in Education* was a finalist in the Associated Writing Program's creative nonfiction competition for 1987.